Getting the Best
of Yourself

Getting
the
Best
of Yourself

DAVID W. AYCOCK

VICTOR BOOKS®

A DIVISION OF SCRIPTURE PRESS PUBLICATIONS INC.
USA CANADA ENGLAND

Scripture quotations are from the *Holy Bible, New International Version,* © 1973, 1978, 1984, International Bible Society. Used by permission of Zondervan Bible Publishers.

Recommended Dewey Decimal Classification: 248.4
Suggested Subject Heading: CHRISTIAN LIVING

Library of Congress Card Catalog Number: 89-60178
ISBN: 0-89693-752-6

VICTOR BOOKS
A division of SP Publications, Inc.
Wheaton, Illinois 60187

Contents

Preface

As a psychologist, I help people through emotional struggles. Over the years, I've discovered some useful strategies for attacking the psychological ills which face us all. I've written this book for Christians who are battling emotional maladies and for those who merely wish to bolster their preventive resources. These strategies are intended to supplement, not replace, God's provisions for us.

The book begins with the premise that God allows emotional upheaval in everyone's life as a result of the Fall. Part I details strategies to cope with the stress which is so much a part of our lives. Techniques include physical exercise, relaxation, thought-stopping, and stress inoculation. In Part II, thinking is the focus. Coping techniques include evaluating circumstances and defining a plan of action. In Part III, we'll look at anger and depression—ways they are related and techniques for managing them. Part IV focuses on getting along with others. I've included tips on effective communication and conflict resolution. Examples in the book from my professional practice have been altered to protect the identity of my clients.

I urge you to read this volume prayerfully and implement the suggestions before you encounter a major stress point. Don't let emotional struggles get the best of you. With God's help you can get the best of yourself.

To my precious daughters,
Kristen and Anna,
who give me countless
hours of joy.

ONE

*"It was good for me to be afflicted so that
I might learn Your decrees."
Psalm 119:71*

Help Yourself

"To do the job right, you must have the right tools." So says an advertisement for a popular tool company. Anyone who tackles a tough job, from the weekend handyman to the professional mechanic, knows the truth of this statement. The angled ratchet extension, the fitted mophead, the wide paintbrush, and the long sewing needle make foreboding tasks more manageable. The right tools eliminate a lot of frustration and wasted time.

Our lives can be compared to great machines. We were designed by a wonderful craftsman, God, and placed in a perfect environment for eternal comfort and joy. Unfortunately, and through no fault of the Designer, our first parents decided to ignore His wishes in favor of self-indulgent activities. Ever since, our "machines" have been prone to malfunction. Luckily, the owner's manual presents the basic solution to these problems, and the Designer Himself performs this critical adjustment for all who request His assistance. But our wiring will not be restored completely until the machines move to another location with the Designer. In the interim we are left with the owner's manual which answers all the fundamental operating questions and suggests principles for specific malfunctions which arise.

Repairing the machine requires right principles and appropriate tools. This book is a hardware store which offers an exciting line of such tools. They are especially helpful in times of mechanical breakdown, but also serve well for those wise persons who engage in preventive maintenance. While a malfunction sometimes requires the hand of a professional mechanic, most of the time a person with a willing mind and ready hands is able to complete the necessary repairs. I trust you'll enjoy your browse through this hardware store, and then take some of these tools with you to keep your machine running smoothly.

Functional Breakdowns Among Christians

Because of the activities of our earliest ancestors, malfunction is an accepted part of our existence; eventual break down is inevitable. Most of us recognize this harsh reality as it relates to physical health each time the flu spreads through our neighborhood or some dust gets in our eyes. But failure is not confined to physical health alone; emotional inner workings are often gummed up as well. In fact, these psychological malfunctions may be more devastating than the physical ones because they are less observable and not as readily accepted.

Even a cursory look at the Scriptures reveals emotional struggles among God's own elite. Job was a contemporary of Abraham; his life is detailed in the oldest book of the Bible. Job was a great man, described by God as "blameless and upright," yet he faced stressful events which would rival any case of twentieth-century burnout. In a matter of days he experienced disasters which claimed the lives of his children, caused financial bankruptcy, and ruined his health. Job's world was turned upside down, and even though he held steadfastly to his faith in God, he was forced to deal with tremendous emotional upheaval. His suffering reveals the entire gamut of negative emotions. In Job 6–7, we see a man in despair. He stated that he was in deep anguish and misery and described his feelings of utter hopelessness (6:2, 11; 7:6). He lamented the undependability of his friends who might offer support and share his loneliness (6:14-15). Job expressed his feelings of futility and the endless insomnia that plagued him in his misery (7:3-4). He exclaimed, "My eyes will never see happiness again" (7:7), a sentiment which often accompanies deep depression. He complained of bitterness, nightmares, and terror (7:11, 14). He concluded that his life had no meaning; he saw his death as the most expedient solution to his ills: "So I prefer strangling and death, rather than this body of mine. I despise my life; I would not live forever. Let me alone; my days have no meaning" (7:15-16).

Job's pain reached into every aspect of his life. Yet, he refused to forsake his Lord or to throw in the towel in his hour of despair. He worked through his problems and was restored to physical and mental health because of this faith and perseverance.

King David was another Old Testament patriarch who understood the meaning of emotional suffering. God acknowledged David as a man after His own heart (Acts 13:22), and yet his life was filled with emotional turmoil. He experienced murderous plots against him by King Saul, a fugitive existence in caves, the rebellion and rivalry of his children which resulted in rape and murder, and agonizing plagues upon himself and his subjects. In Psalm 6, David expressed his emotional struggles resulting from a physical illness. He stated that he was faint and in agony, that his soul was in anguish, and that he was worn out from groaning and weeping (6:2-3, 6). When his son Absalom conspired against him, David cried to the Lord that he was distraught, his heart in anguish and overwhelmed with fear, trembling, and horror (Psalm 55:2, 4-5). David underwent severe emotional turmoil and reported that he was scorned, disgraced, and shamed by his enemies. He felt heartbroken and helpless, but found no comforters (Psalm 69:19-20). These passages and countless others demonstrate the mental strife that often faced this hero of the faith.

Jesus' own disciples walked daily with their Master but were not spared from fear. Terrifying storms still arose on the sea when the disciples and Jesus traveled by boat (Mark 4:35-41). Peter's mother-in-law was not immune from illness (Luke 4:38-39) even though Peter frequently healed many on his journeys for Christ. The disciples argued among themselves about their status with the Saviour, and when the mother of James and John requested special recognition of her sons, the other ten disciples were indignant (Matthew 20:24). The apostles harbored a traitor in their own band, and all forsook Jesus when the authorities apprehended him. Their walk with Christ could hardly be characterized as worry-free.

Likewise, the Apostle Paul led anything but a stress-free life. In his letter to the Corinthian Christians, he recounted his personal experiences as the apostle to the Gentiles:

> *Five times I received from the Jews the forty lashes minus one. Three times I was beaten with rods, once I was stoned, three times I was shipwrecked. I spent a night and a day in the open sea. I have been constantly on the move. I have been in danger from rivers, in danger from bandits, in danger from my own countrymen, in danger from Gentiles; in danger in the city; in danger in the country, in danger at sea; and in danger from false brothers. I have labored and toiled and have often gone without sleep; I have known hunger and thirst and have often gone without food; I have been cold and naked. Besides everything else, I face daily the pressure of my concern for all the churches. (2 Corinthians 11:24-28)*

Emotional turmoil strikes both Christians and non-Christians, for suffering is part of the human condition. Unfortunately, many Christians choose to ignore biblical references to negative emotions; instead, they attribute any struggle to the personal unrighteousness or faithlessness of the sufferer. Such pronouncements of guilt to a hurting person only serve to intensify the struggle. Holding these ideas prevents people from acknowledging their difficulties

to God, themselves, or others. Such denial serves to perpetuate their problems.

Purposes for Emotional Struggles

The notion that psychological problems are consequences
of sin or unfaithfulness to God is not a new one. Historically, humans have viewed illness and distress as visitations
from unhappy gods, and have offered sacrifices of posses-
sions and human lives to appease these deities and stay
sentences of divine judgment.

Because Jesus often encountered this thinking, He addressed the issue directly. On being told about some Galile-
ans who were massacred by Pilate, Jesus said that their
suffering was not attributable to their excessive sinfulness
and could have befallen anyone in His audience. He then
pointed to a recent tragedy—the toppling of a tower which
claimed the lives of eighteen people—and declared that
these victims were no more guilty of unrighteousness than
any others living in Jerusalem. He emphasized that all persons were susceptible to suffering and death and, therefore, in need of repentance and atonement for alleviation
of the eternal consequences of sin (Luke 13).

Jesus faced questions from His own disciples about the
issue of suffering for sinful behavior when they encountered a man who had been born blind. The disciples asked,
"Rabbi, who sinned, this man or his parents, that he was
born blind?" (John 9:2) They assumed, as did the Jewish
leaders, that this affliction was a result of unrighteousness.
Jesus, however, contradicted this assumption: "Neither this
man nor his parents sinned, but this happened so that the
work of God might be displayed in his life" (v. 3).

All human suffering is the result of original sin—
humankind's rejection of God's perfect plan for their lives
and His rules developed to sustain this plan. Had Adam and
Eve not rebelled against God, sin, death, and suffering
would not exist. The destructive consequences of the fall
of humankind inherently affect all persons. To look for
specific individual sins as determinants of any malady is

sheer folly. We all know of tragedies that befall God-fearing people, while multiple successes enrich the lives of the godless. King David regularly bemoaned these inequities as he watched God's enemies prosper while the righteous languished. Job asked the question, "Why do the righteous suffer?" When Job's comforters insisted that his problems were penalties for his sin, God became angry with them for their insensitivity in accusing their upright brother. We too must reject this simplistic explanation for emotional problems.

Emotional trials are always uncomfortable but rarely without meaning. In my professional practice of psychology, I regularly see patients who are beset with all types of emotional troubles. Their problems range from excessive anxiety to energy-sapping depression. But just as physical pain signals a breakdown in the body's organ systems, so negative emotions can alert a person to unhealthy thinking, inappropriate behaviors, or unresolved psychological issues. Excessive anxiety may help identify a stressful lifestyle. Depression may stem from negative thinking or marital difficulties. Nightmares can arise from past trauma with which one has never dealt. Sometimes these emotional symptoms become more problematic than the situations which underlie them; yet, they usually point our attention to a trouble spot. The feelings are so uncomfortable that they provide the necessary motivation to change a thinking process or misbehavior that would otherwise go unchecked. David declares this use of suffering: "It was good for me to be afflicted so that I might learn Your decrees" (Psalm 119:71).

God allows difficulties into our lives to provide opportunities for emotional and spiritual growth. James, the pastor of the early church in Jerusalem, wrote, "Consider it pure joy, my brothers, whenever you face trials of many kinds, because you know that the testing of your faith develops perseverance" (James 1:2-3). The Apostle Paul noted that the Lord refused to remove a tormenting "thorn in the flesh" in order to prevent conceit in the evangelist, and also to display His power continually in Paul's life (2 Corinthians 12:7-10). Emotional hardships can give us a frame of reference to appreciate better the less stressful times. It is easy to become complacent when day-to-day existence requires little coping effort.

Emotional pain also prepares us to minister to others. Paul declares:

> *Praise be to the God and Father of our Lord Jesus Christ, the Father of compassion and the God of all comfort, who comforts us in all our troubles, so that we can comfort those in any trouble with the comfort we ourselves had received from God. (2 Corinthians 1:3-4)*

Apparently God allows some distress to enter our lives so that we can experience the pain and His comfort. This enables us to minister God's comfort more realistically to others.

Maintenance

Regardless of the purpose for emotional struggles, they are draining and demand much attention. Acknowledging their presence is the first step in understanding and managing them. Once Christians are willing to accept the presence of emotional difficulties, without berating themselves for excessive sinfulness, they can initiate the process of working through the feelings. This acknowledgment is sometimes the most difficult step in the process.

Sometimes in a social situation, people will approach a psychologist to discuss a personal problem under the guise of gaining information to assist a friend. I well remember the time a young single woman approached me after church, reporting that she had a friend in deep distress. Angela gave a detailed description and history of her "friend's" problem and asked for advice which she might pass along. I asked a few questions to gain further information and Angela's quick and thorough replies left little doubt that her forlorn "friend" was conversing with me at that moment.

Angela's situation demanded more attention than a consultation in a public place could afford, so I asked her to visit me at my office. She admitted that indeed she was the distressed person, but said that she could not seek professional help because others might view this as evidence of unrighteousness. Angela never did work through her struggles. When I saw her later, she claimed that the problems were not as bad as she had earlier thought and were not interfering with her present lifestyle. The painful truth was that Angela's difficulties were obvious to those around her; her unwillingness to acknowledge their presence only deepened their hold on her.

Many Angelas populate evangelical churches. They muddle around in their dysfunctional lifestyles because they will not acknowledge glaring emotional malfunctions which are easily noticed by all those around.

● Divine tools. After acknowledging the existence of an emotion struggle, the repair work can begin. The tools are both divine and human. God cares about His children and asks us to exercise faith in His grand scheme for our lives. Faith is a tricky tool to master because it often does not operate as we expect. While he wasted away in an Egyptian jail, Joseph must have wondered how he would ever rule over his brothers. Likewise, we sometimes find it difficult to exercise faith when it's not clear how our emotional or situational imprisonment is fulfilling any meaningful purpose.

Questioning God about the turmoil in our lives is nothing new. Dozens of biblical characters wondered aloud about personal life events which did not appear to expedite their welfare or God's best interest. Balaam beat his donkey mercilessly when the beast wouldn't carry him where he wanted to go. However, when the prophet's eyes were opened to the angel with a drawn sword in the path, he gained an appreciation for his donkey's strange behavior.

We too may doubt God's interest when events don't go

the way we wish. But this is often because we are blind to His grand scheme for our lives. Seeing the big picture as God does clarifies our use of the Faith tool.

• Psychological tools. Other tools in the repair shop are psychological in nature. They aren't substitutes for the divine tools, but rather they complement them nicely. Indeed, God prescribes them throughout the Scriptures to treat emotional problems. The Bible is an instructional manual and gives authoritative directions on coping with anger, managing anxiety, and opening communication channels with others.

However, the main theme of the Scriptures is God's master plan of salvation for all people. The Bible was never intended to be a comprehensive psychological text. In places in which God's revelation touches on a particular discipline, His Word is trustworthy. But there are many facets of psychology and other human endeavors on which God has not spoken specifically. Instead, He has created our minds with vast capabilities, and He allows us to learn about ourselves and develop strategies for mental wellness. As such, wholeness and holiness are not in opposition but are, rather, complementary. Although the Bible outlines general guidelines for psychological understanding and change, it does not always detail the specific steps to mental health. When cultural psychological propositions come into clear conflict with scriptural revelation, obviously the Bible takes precedence. But this conflict occurs less often than most Christians presume.

The objections of some conservative Christians to professional psychology often amaze me. Even though we don't find detailed descriptions in the pages of Scripture of the medical techniques used to perform a heart transplant or even to set a broken arm, few would label these procedures unbiblical. Psychological techniques such as communication training or thought modification are biblical in principle. Not all psychologists or doctors are Christians, but then God never limited discovery of truth only to believers. Many non-Christians learn to use the brain created in God's image in ways that benefit everyone.

We cannot afford to ignore the advances of psychological research. Just as we routinely use computers to print Bibles and use our understanding of tax codes to attract donors to our Christian ministry, so we can equip ourselves with psychological sophistication for maximum health and personal growth.

SECTION 1

We live in an age of excessive stress and anxiety. It seems that the only constant in our society is change. Technology progresses so rapidly that new developments are often obsolete before they can filter down from the scientific research journals to the popular press. Innovations in transportation and information processing have made the world much more accessible and have placed knowledge at our fingertips like never before in human history. But these advancements have not come without consequences.

As the merry-go-round speeds up, we find it more difficult to stay on our horses. The choices are often overwhelming, and our relationships with one another frequently suffer.

Stress has been linked to a wide range of physical illnesses, including coronary heart disease, cancer, and stroke—the degenerative diseases which are the three leading causes of death for Americans. Excessive stress and anxiety also contribute to emotional disorders and reduce the quality of life considerably.

Christians inhabit the same stressful world that non-Christians occupy, with its global conflicts, domestic ills, and daily hassles. The strategies described in this section are physical and psychological measures helpful in reducing stress and anxiety. I hope that they will aid you in combating this significant threat to your health and happiness.

TWO

*"You were bought at a price. There-
fore honor God with your body."
1 Corinthians 6:20*

Get Moving!

Stress produces very real physical effects. Remember a time while driving when you suddenly came on an object in the road? Maybe you were rounding a curve only to find an animal scampering across the highway or a stalled car in the road. You probably coped with this stressor by swerving to avoid the object or slamming the brake pedal to the floor. But how did you feel afterward? You may have noticed that your knees were weak, your heart beat faster, you perspired more than usual, and you were more alert to road conditions than before. These feelings are all physical consequences of stress.

These physical symptoms occur whenever we face stressful or traumatic situations. Most people fear public speaking and are quite aware of the muscle tension, accelerated heart rate, and concentration difficulties when they face an audience whose eyes and ears are focused on them. New experiences often produce this physical stress response as well. Most of us can remember the uneasiness of our bodies on a first date or when starting a new job.

The Physiology of Stress and Anxiety
God's design of the human body is magnificent. The body is expertly crafted to operate for decades, regulate its in-

ternal functions, detect problems as they arise, and provide self-maintenance for restoration.

The body's response to stressors is no exception. Although we generally dislike the anxious feelings and physical discomfort that arise when we are under stress, a closer examination of the body's reaction reveals a carefully orchestrated symphony of organ systems working in concert to protect us from harm. Whenever a threat is registered in our brains, a complex neurological and hormonal network is readied for action. The body prepares itself to run or fight. Consider how you respond to stress and see if you recognize these bodily changes:

● The pupils of your eyes dilate to allow more light to enter. This helps you see your stressor more clearly.

● You breathe faster and deeper to pull more oxygen into the body.

● Your blood sugar level rises as sugar stored around the body deposit their contents into the bloodstream, and fats and proteins are also dumped into the blood for conversion to sugar in the event that more energy is needed.

● Now that you have this extra oxygen and sugar in the blood, your internal transportation system swings into high gear. Your heart begins to beat more rapidly to rush these nutrients to the various muscle groups where the action will be initiated.

● Your blood pressure rises because of changes in the size of the blood vessels around your kidneys, and now your blood is moving faster and at a higher pressure as it circulates throughout the body. Indeed, you may even have expressed this phenomenon by saying that someone stressful makes your blood pressure rise.

● Your muscles tense as they prepare for action. This tension, if prolonged, may put pressure on nerve endings around the muscle, resulting in pain; thus the expression, "He's a pain in the neck."

● You begin to perspire as your speeded-up body releases a coolant for temperature regulation.

● Your digestive processes slow down as blood moves

from concentrations in the internal organs to the various muscle groups.

● Your skin blanches as blood leaves the areas around your skin and moves into the muscles. This is one of the reasons you are more susceptible to rashes and other skin eruptions in times of excessive stress.

These changes quickly mobilize the body to run or fight, and this is important if the stressor you face is physically threatening. God designed the human body with this system for self-protection.

Most of the events which cause stress for us are not physically threatening. We experience stress from social sources, like interpersonal hassles with friends and family members. Stress also arises from psychological sources. We often set unrealistic standards for ourselves and berate ourselves when we don't meet them. We refuse to turn off our negative thinking and suffer stress as a result. Our modern environment produces plenty of stressors as well. Work deadlines face us daily and traffic jams abound.

For most of our stressors, running or fighting may not be appropriate responses. If your spouse says something stressful to you, you could slug him. But this would hardly be biblical and it would do little to promote marital harmony. You might run out of your boss' office when she scolds you, but this immature action would probably contribute further to your stress. The fact is, most of the time when stress arouses us, our bodies prepare us for the wrong action. Instead of calming us down to develop a rational response, we become keyed up and more likely to act without forethought. Our muscles are geared up to do something, but we don't need their assistance. Our physical responses are often as problematic to us as is the original stressor, and now we must contend with two adversaries instead of one.

After emergency mobilization is triggered, stress products may remain in the bloodstream for up to an hour before they are reabsorbed. Additional stress results in another initiation of the fight/flight response, prolonging the

chemical upheaval. The emotional consequence of this pro-
liferation of stress hormones is quite evident to us, just as
it is to those around us. Excessive stress makes us anxious
and increases worry and nervousness. We're more irritable
and tend to be critical and discouraging in our comments
to others. We may become restless and have difficulty falling asleep or remaining asleep through the night.

Chronic stress also interferes with concentration and
narrows perception. When we're under stress, it's difficult
to focus on a task, especially if there is noise or distraction.
In order to complete a job, we steer all concentration to a
relatively small and manageable area and we miss the big
picture. Maybe this is why the task of completing income
tax forms is so arduous and stressful. The instructions are
usually complicated and our anxious arousal makes it difficult to concentrate. This combination contributes to misin-
terpretations of the instructions and ensuing feelings of
being overwhelmed and helpless. These emotions engender
more stress, and the cycle continues.

Besides the immediate physical consequences of
stress—emergency mobilization—and the negative emotions it produces, prolonged stress can have devastating
effects on our health. Chronic stress contributes to coronary heart disease, strokes, and other circulatory problems
as the mobilization process encourages the admittance into
the bloodstream of fats which clog the arteries. Blood pressure elevations during the fight/flight response promote hy-
pertension. Over time the rerouting of the blood from the
stomach to the muscles may cause peptic ulcers and other
gastrointestinal problems. Prolonged stress inhibits the
body's immune response and makes it more susceptible to
infection and cancer. Stress has been implicated in many
other illnesses including asthma, tension and migraine
headaches, lower-back pain, and sexual dysfunctions.

If You Can't Beat 'Em, Join 'Em

A typical reaction to the identification of the physical and
emotional effects of stress is discouragement. The list of

problems seems overwhelming and stress is not likely to disappear from our fast-paced culture. Just what can we do to avoid these pitfalls of modern life?

Why not do what our bodies have prepared us to do? If our neurological and hormonal systems have devoted such an effort to prepare us to run or fight, maybe we should go along with the plan. The quickest way to rid ourselves of these stress hormones and prevent them from unleashing their forces against our health is to burn them up through physical activity. If you're dressed in a swimsuit, you don't try to attend a formal dinner. Why should you ignore the function your body has dressed you to attend?

Much of the time we disregard muscle tension and then wonder why we feel more anxious and irritable or have trouble concentrating. Many Americans seek to expend energy vicariously by sitting in an easy chair and watching athletes compete. Unfortunately, this does not work. In fact, researchers have shown that the physical arousal levels of the nonparticipants (coaches and fans) at athletic events is much higher than that of the players themselves. This is not because the nonparticipants care more about the outcome, but rather because they have no means of dissipating the stress chemicals from the bloodstream.

The "running and fighting" which burns up stress products may take many forms. Actual running or fighting would satisfy the requirements, but they are not always appropriate. Any activity which demands movement of the muscles will suffice. The more vigorous the activity, the more adrenaline is consumed. Walking, climbing stairs, lifting weights, doing push-ups—even moving furniture—are effective stress reducers. If your job is stressful, you would be better served by taking a walk at lunchtime than by sitting in a restaurant for the entire hour. I often advise students to take five to ten minutes of each stressful study hour for some physical activity in order to aid concentration and retention of material.

I lived in Indiana for five years and often found the frigid winters to be very stressful. The native Hoosiers seemed acclimated to the climate and although most would admit their discomfort with frigid temperatures, high winds, and deep snowdrifts, they handled it routinely as a natural aspect of human existence. As a native Southerner, I viewed the winter's cruelty with much less objectivity and much more disdain. I interpreted below-zero temperatures as a threat to my existence and as an unnecessary obstacle to my personal happiness. The mere mention of that dreaded four-letter word *snow* engendered a good deal of anxiety in me.

However, I soon found that snowstorms demand a physical action which lowers stress levels significantly. The snow had a very bad habit of accumulating at the same depth over my entire yard—including my driveway. This required using the snow shovel, a physical activity which demands enormous stores of energy for successful operation. While I never learned to appreciate snow on any land mass other than a ski slope, I always had the means to burn up the stress introduced by the unwelcomed element.

Regular Exercise

Since physical activity is so effective in reducing stress and anxiety, we need to identify some means of physical exertion to employ when the tension builds. Almost any actions that expend energy are helpful in burning up the harmful stress products. However, the unpredictability of our daily stressors and the frequent constraints to immediate physical activity confront us with a problem. We may be inundated with stressors from unexpected sources such as advanced deadlines, pop quizzes, absences of coworkers, or the illness of a child and find ourselves unable to deal with these frustrations through physical activity. We can't always respond to our boss by saying, "Hold on. Your criticism of my work requires twenty-five push-ups to help me cope." Indeed, the only actions that may seem rational at that moment probably fall outside the realm of appropriate behaviors.

Therefore, we need a regular program of rhythmic bodily

actions which use our dominant muscles. There's no way around it—we need to *exercise*. This fact does not routinely engender excitement from anxious clients in psychotherapy or participants in my stress management workshops. Exercise lacks the sophistication of psychological strategies for handling problematic emotions and disappoints those who want a quick fix to stress.

Objections to exercise as an anxiety management strategy are legion. I hear them from my clients and workshop participants regularly: "I'm under too much stress now, and I don't have the energy to exercise.... Exercise increases my appetite and makes me overeat.... I tried exercising once and I never learned to enjoy it."

Exercise meets needs in the body. It uses up stress products and gives us energy instead of sapping it. It relieves stress and aids our mental concentration. Regular exercise has been shown to *reduce* appetite. Nobody said exercising was a carnival of fun, but neither is coping with heart disease.

Since the Bible is not a physiological textbook, it is not surprising that it says little about exercise. However, we know that exercise is an important aspect of maintaining the body. The Apostle Paul reminds us that the body is the temple of the Holy Spirit, bought with a price, and that we are to glorify God in our physical choices (1 Corinthians 6:19-20). Paul must have been a sportsman, given the frequent athletic analogies he uses to describe the Christian life. In his epistles to Timothy, Paul likens a godly witness to a boxing match (1 Timothy 6:12), exhorts this young pastor to be strong and fair in ministry like a successful athlete (2 Timothy 2:5) and compares his long years of service to the Lord to a good fight and successful race for which he will receive a victor's crown (2 Timothy 4:7-8).

Paul uses the analogy of training for athletic events to encourage the Corinthians to engage in godly behaviors (1 Corinthians 9:24-27). Some have used Paul's words to Timothy to minimize the importance of exercise. But a careful look at the passage reveals that Paul held physical training in high regard, but spiritual growth much higher: "For physical training is of some value, but godliness has value for all things, holding promise for both the present life and the life to come" (1 Timothy 4:8). While the Scriptures do not specifically mandate physical exercise, they exhort us to maintain our bodies for the most effective service.

Aerobic Exercise

Any physical activity which demands action by the mobilized muscles will burn stress chemicals and reduce anxiety. But some methods of energy expenditure are more beneficial to the body than are others. Aerobic exercise is king of the physical fitness hill. *Aerobic* means "exercising within your breath," that is, physical activity adjusted to your body's ability to supply adequate oxygen to the muscles. The heart itself is a muscle which pumps oxygen and other vital resources to all body cells. The only way the heart muscle can be built up is through regularly exercising it and gradually increasing the demand for better performance. As Hippocrates said, "That which is used develops, and that which is not used wastes away." To build your biceps, you force them into action by lifting weights. To build your heart, you force it into action by walking, jogging, cycling, or swimming—any exercise which calls for sustained, rhythmic movements of the body's dominant muscles.

The benefits of aerobic exercise are tremendous. Besides dissipating stress products and strengthening the heart muscle, aerobic exercise increases lung efficiency, improves the blood supply to the heart, enhances capillary growth, stimulates the production of hemoglobin (the blood's oxygen carriers), decreases the lining of the blood vessels enlarged by cholesterol, and reduces blood pressure. Regular aerobic exercise burns calories and gives more energy. In addition to anxiety reduction, other psychological effects include enhanced self-esteem, an improved mental outlook, and increased motivation and self-discipline. It is hard to imagine a more profitable activity for your health.

• Determining your training range. You need not be a Boston marathon contestant to engage in aerobic exercise. You don't even have to run. However, you do have to elevate your heart rate through use of your large muscles in a rhythmic, repetitive, continuous motion for at least twenty minutes three times a week or more.

How much faster should you make your heart beat? The answer depends on your age. You need to keep your heart rate in a *training range* to achieve an aerobic effect. Your personal training range can be computed using the following formula:

220 minus your age x 70% = your lower limit

220 minus your age x 85% = your upper limit

To exercise your heart muscle most efficiently, you should keep it beating in this range for a minimum of twenty consecutive minutes. For example, if your age is forty, your training range would be calculated as follows:

220−40 = 180 x 70% = 126 (your lower limit)

220−40 = 180 x 85% = 153 (your upper limit)

You must find an exercise which elevates your heart rate between 126 and 153 beats a minute and in which you can engage continuously for at least twenty minutes. As you can see, the older you are, the lower the demands you must make on your heart.

• Choosing the right aerobic exercise. You need to choose aerobic exercise which fits your personal needs and tastes. Some people enjoy activities which take them out of doors like walking, jogging, or swimming. Some find it easier to use an aerobic workout tape, and still others prefer sports such as basketball or handball.

You should take a few things into consideration as you choose. Determine how convenient the exercise will be for you. Walking, jogging, or cycling can be done alone and with little planning. Engaging in an organized sport requires coordinating your schedule with that of others. Joining a racquetball club involves a good deal of money; purchasing a jump rope is inexpensive. Unless you live in a warm climate, weather conditions may interfere with your scheduled aerobics. A jogging trampoline or stationary bike for home use will always provide you with an indoor alternative. Exercising with a friend is mutually encouraging, so find a partner who can join you in your activity to add extra motivation.

Remember—you need only maintain your heart rate in your training range, not prepare for the Olympics. For persons who are older or out of shape, walking should easily accomplish the desired effect. As you become more physically fit, you may need to walk more briskly or graduate to a more strenuous activity. Base the decisions for these changes on your body's response, not your desire for athletic acclaim.

It is wise to consult a physician before embarking on an aerobic exercise program if you have any illness or reason to believe that it might endanger your health. Always take time to warm up before beginning your full exercise routine and take time to cool down slowly after you finish. Your warm-up time will help you increase your pulse slowly so that you are at your training range when you begin your exercise.

THREE

"When anxiety was great within me,
Your consolation brought joy to my soul."
Psalm 94:19

Stop That Thinking!

From time to time we all have trouble shaking stressful thoughts. It could be something as simple as a nagging internal voice which keeps asking, "Are you sure you turned the stove off before you left the house?" that keeps us from totally enjoying an evening out. As parents, we know what happens when we hear a slight noise coming from the room of a sleeping child; in a few minutes we decide we must visit the child's bedroom. Or, perhaps we're already in bed when we begin to question whether the front door is locked. It's amazing how rarely the stove is left on, the kids are in distress, or the front door is unlocked, but our inability to stop wondering creates a good deal of anxiety.

Sometimes, the thoughts you can't seem to drop are those which replay stressful life experiences. You repetitively relive the embarrassment of making a critical remark about Joe, only to turn around and see him standing behind you. You may say to yourself, "What a stupid thing to say. Surely he didn't hear me." Perhaps you ruminate over that exam question which seemed impossible during the test, but now, after reviewing the chapter again, seems so answerable. Or maybe you can't get the statement that you heard this morning from Marge out of your head. How you wish you would have replied with the response that seems so appropriate now, instead of the unimaginative one you used. Think of all the stress you could eliminate if you could turn back the hands of time!

Most of our anxiety originates between our ears; it's not our environment that upsets us as much as our interpretation of that environment. This became very clear to me when I left Atlanta to direct the counseling services of a small Christian college in rural Indiana. Contrasts between the two areas were immediately apparent to me—population, accents, etc. But one difference wasn't evident until my first Indiana November when a cold white substance began to fall from the sky. And not only did it fall, but it had the audacity to stick to the ground, even the road. Well, this Southerner had witnessed a snowfall before, so I knew exactly what to do—turn the radio on for all of the obligatory cancellations. However, I was amazed to discover that this climatic disturbance was hardly newsworthy— there was no mention of any shutdowns. I would have to risk my life to go to work!

I had never driven in the snow and had little desire to learn. I still remember my troublesome thoughts while sitting behind the steering wheel of my car that morning: "This is horrible! How can they expect me to go to work in these conditions? I'm on the other side of town from the college. Well, okay, so it is only a mile and a half, but it's still dangerous. I could slide into the ditch and freeze in this weather before help arrived. I could die."

With these troublesome thoughts filling my mind, I journeyed toward my work at the safe pace of fifteen miles an hour, hands tightly gripping the steering wheel, leaning forward with all alertness. Other motorists seemed to approach me very rapidly and most ventured around me with little effort. It was amazing. The same road conditions existed for both me and the native northern drivers, but I *interpreted* the snow very differently. My stressful self-statements determined my mood. Their constant repetition on the airwaves of my mind resulted in increased worry and escalation of stress until I talked myself into a harrowing experience. It was only after I stopped my fatalistic thinking that I learned to drive on the snow and ice.

Obsessive Thoughts

Troubling thoughts which we cannot terminate are called *"obsessions"* and produce an enormous amount of anxiety. Obsessions have plagued human beings throughout recorded history. The Bible chronicles numerous accounts of persons who were preoccupied with stressful thoughts. The Jewish leaders of Jesus' day were so obsessed with their desire to dispose of the Christ that they arrested Him without provocation, tried Him illegally, condemned Him to death unjustly, and incited the masses to support their sentence unmercifully. In this same fashion the Pharisee, Saul (who was later converted and renamed Paul), vehemently pursued and persecuted first-century believers. In his defense before King Agrippa, Paul characterized his preoccupation with this task as "my obsession" (Acts 26:11).

Obsessions can be very costly in terms of human suffering and in some instances have been fatal. Such was the case with Haman whose tragic story is unfolded in the Book of Esther. Haman was the most honored nobleman in Persia under King Xerxes during a time that many Israelites lived in exile in that country. Everyone paid homage to Haman except for Mordecai, a devout Jew who did not believe in worshiping men, regardless of their political station. Haman became so incensed with Mordecai's refusal to kneel to him that he could not enjoy the respect he received from others. He became so obsessed with the idea of disposing of Mordecai that this anxiety-producing thought ruled his existence. He even plotted the eradication of all the Jewish people to secure his revenge. On the very day that Haman had a gallows constructed for the execution of Mordecai, Queen Esther invited Haman to a banquet at the palace and exposed his wickedness. Haman's obsession resulted in the king's edict to hang Haman on his own newly built gallows.

Obsessions can haunt several members of the same family. Such was the case with King David. Second Samuel 11–12 record David's illicit liaison with Bathsheba and his subsequent murder of her husband, Uriah. David's sexual obsession resulted in the death of a child and turmoil in his kingdom. This obsession, modeled so clearly by the king, wrecked the lives of his children as well. David's son, Amnon, became obsessed "to the point of illness" with the desire to have sexual relations with his half sister, Tamar. Amnon tricked Tamar into a sexual encounter and was later murdered for his impropriety by Tamar's full brother, Absalom. Obsessive thoughts can lead to alarming actions.

Obsessions may lead to pathological behaviors as well. King Saul was overtaken with such jealousy over David's popularity and with paranoia about fears of David's plans to overthrow him that he threw javelins at David and then hunted him like a fugitive. When repetitive behaviors accompany obsessive thoughts, they are said to be *obsessive compulsive*. Perhaps the most famous of these is Shakespeare's Lady MacBeth who to no avail constantly washed her hands in an effort to cleanse them of her murderous deed.

The anxiety produced by obsessive thinking causes us to lose sight of the big picture and focus instead on stressful details. This anxiety can result in a loss of control as we amble about with tunnel vision, failing to consider the full range of alternatives available to us. Like Captain Ahab in *Mobey Dick*, we endanger our own lives and those of our whole crew by chasing an elusive white whale and disregarding our broader mission, to hunt whales. Obsessive thinking also hampers us by repeatedly eliciting the stress response as our bodies gear up for mobilization each time the worry arises anew.

God's Perspective on Troubling Thoughts
The Bible addresses anxiety-inducing thoughts in several places and consistently warns against this unproductive use of our energy. Jesus cautioned His disciples to refrain

from preoccupation with food and clothes and to eliminate worry from their daily practice. Likewise, David reiterated the admonition, "Do not fret," three times in the initial eight verses of Psalm 37. He specified the uselessness of worrying about the apparent immunity from the consequences of their deeds that evil men enjoy. He then warned that excessive fretting over these inequities could cause us to act sinfully.

God's perspective is always an eternal one. Unfortunately, ours is much more limited. Paul wrote to the Corinthian Christians: "So we fix our eyes not on what is seen, but on what is unseen. For what is seen is temporary, but what is unseen is eternal" (2 Corinthians 4:18). Paul mastered this eternal focus to the extent that while in prison he could write, "I have learned to be content whatever the circumstances" (Philippians 4:11). Often our faith is much like that of the father from whose son Jesus exorcised an evil spirit. He expressed his wavering faith truthfully when he told Jesus, "I do believe; help me overcome my unbelief!" (Mark 9:24)

God's antidote for anxious thinking is to hand your worry over to Him. Peter implores, "Cast all your anxiety on Him (God) because He cares for you" (1 Peter 5:7). Likewise, Paul exhorts us, "Do not be anxious about anything, but in everything, by prayer and petition, with thanksgiving, present your requests to God" (Philippians 4:6). Jesus invites us, "Come to Me, all you who are weary and burdened, and I will give you rest" (Matthew 11:28). David declares the results of this strategy: "When anxiety was great within me, Your consolation brought joy to my soul" (Psalm 94:19).

Most Christians have no arguments with the efficacy of God's promise to comfort us when we're anxious. We would love to deliver all anxiety over to Him. The problem lies in the transfer process. It is usually difficult to make a clean handoff even though our halfback never fumbles. We're the ones that have trouble letting go. We need a strategy to terminate our unproductive worrying.

Thought-Stopping

Psychologists have long recognized the stressfulness of negative thinking. Stressful thinking is a major reason many people enter psychotherapy. Sometimes insight alone into the irrational aspects of distressing thoughts is enough to help people terminate them. But more often specific training in the process of thought elimination is necessary. One of the most basic and effective strategies for this outcome is called *thought-stopping*. It has four components: detecting stressful thoughts, imagining the thoughts, interrupting the thoughts, and replacing the thoughts.

• Detecting stressful thoughts. It may seem rather obvious, but we must identify our stressful thoughts before we can eliminate them. In many cases this is easy. The student who is looking at an examination question on a topic she never studied knows full well why she feels anxious. The driver of a car who is being escorted to the shoulder of the road by the blinking lights of a highway patrolman has no difficulty identifying the precipitator of his elevated heart rate. Similarly, the pregnant woman entering the delivery room can quickly tell you why she is not relaxed. In these cases, anxious thinking is easy to detect because people universally relate to these events with a noticeable amount of stress.

Unrealistic thinking is often more difficult to notice. One detection strategy is to examine our experiences at the time the anxious thinking began. Several years ago Sheila, a college student, consulted me because she was having panic attacks and couldn't control her anxiety. She reported that while walking from her car to her office building in the mornings, she often felt overwhelmed with thoughts of impending danger. She tried to give these feelings over to God, but to no avail. I first investigated with her whether there were any physical dangers during this walk; she knew of none. Then, we looked at the time period in which the troublesome thinking began and this investigation was more fruitful. Sheila pinpointed the morning that the problem started and after careful consideration of the events surrounding that morning, she discovered the source of her anxious thinking. She once fainted in public as a child and this frightened her tremendously. On the onset morning she felt a little dizzy on her way to the office and even stumbled as she walked through the parking lot. From that chance occurrence, Sheila began associating the parking lot with the fear of lying unconscious and out of control in public. After discovering this anxious thought, a plan was devised which included thought-stopping as an important part of her treatment.

Another way to detect stressful thinking is to use the anxiety itself as a cue to examine your most recent thoughts. As you work backward repeatedly from the anxiety to the thinking, common themes often emerge which contain the negative thoughts. This is the method I used with Bill, a fifty-eight-year-old man who was referred to me by his boss after he had several spells of uncontrollable crying at work. Bill had never struggled with excessive anxiety in the past and couldn't understand his current problems. His life seemed well in order and he reported that he did not know what precipitated his emotional outbursts. For a homework assignment I asked him to use his anxiety as a signal to record the stream of thoughts which immediately preceded his crying. His detective work uncovered a common theme—thoughts of different family members were present in every case. Bill then noted that he was very concerned about his children and grandchildren and although he knew of no threats to any of them, he feared for their safety. Bill learned to turn his cares over to the Lord and used thought-stopping to terminate his negative thinking.

Detection of stressful thoughts is essential if we are to deliver our anxieties to God. We can be sure that all anxiety results from some internal conversations we are having with ourselves. Identifying the thought patterns through considering their onset, working back from the anxiety to the thinking, or other methods such as prayer is the first step in eliminating them.

● Imagining the thoughts. Once we identify a stressful thought, we must concentrate on it fully. This may seem like an odd assignment since the ultimate goal is to stop the thinking; but any military tactician will inform you that a thorough understanding of the enemy is essential to defeating him on the battlefield. Thought-stopping can be very intense war on the battlefield of the mind.

Try to determine every aspect of the anxiety-producing thought. Identify its major premises and each related corollary idea. For example, let's assume that after successful cancer surgery, Sue continues to worry that she will die prematurely of cancer. Even though physicians assure her that her health is fine, her anxiety still persists. She focuses on her body continuously and mentally magnifies the slightest ache or pain. She points to Great-aunt Nettie, who contracted terminal cancer, as evidence that she has a genetic predisposition to this disease. At the same time she discounts the fact that no closer relatives battled with this health problem. Sue constantly prays, turning her fears over to God and straightforwardly snatches them back as soon as she says "Amen." She is under constant, self-induced stress.

Sue must recognize her stressful thinking and the pattern by which it typically proceeds. She may first notice some discomfort in a part of her body, and that focus will exaggerate the feeling. Then she considers her own bout with cancer and compares the sensations. She always detects some commonalities and then remembers poor Aunt Nettie. She prays with little expectation of God's comfort; yet, she wants His relief desperately. Sue now has her anxiety-producing thinking pattern well in mind.

● Interrupting the thoughts. Step three requires a quick and decisive termination of the stressful thinking. In psychological textbooks, the usual method for thought interruption is to shout "STOP!" A loud shout usually arrests our attention. This thought interruption is prescribed *every time* the stressful thought is detected, regardless of time or place of occurrence.

I find that most people are unwilling to risk social embarrassment by shouting "STOP!" (or anything else, for that matter) while in public. Stressful thinking which warrants thought-stopping usually arises repeatedly in short time spans, and few people will scream their interruptions at their work stations or in a crowded mall, or even in the presence of sympathetic family members.

For these reasons I suggest a quieter thought interruption method. The placement of a rubber band around the wrist is an effective alternative. Greet the occurrence of a stressful thought with a pop on the wrist by the rubber band and a strong but quiet command to "STOP!" The wrist pop should produce only slight pain; its purpose is to direct your attention away from stressful thinking to other stimuli (the sensation on your arm and the internal message to stop), not to punish or harm yourself.

Practice is very helpful in mastering this strategy. When stressful thinking begins, set a timer to ring in a minute or less. Then purposefully engage in your stressful thoughts until the timer signals you to pop your wrist and command yourself to stop. This time span is realistic in that you are usually well into your negative thinking before you realize it.

Ultimately, you want to interrupt these stressful thoughts as they arise naturally. Whenever you discover any portion of the bad thinking during your normal course of activities, immediately pop and stop, even if this requires repeated action in very short spans of time.

• Replacing the thoughts. The final step in thought-stopping is replacing the stressful ideas with more functional ones. It is very difficult merely to empty our minds completely. We seem always to talk to ourselves. Anxious thoughts are like bad habits—they return as soon as we let our guard down. Failure to introduce a suitable substitute will leave the door open for the worrisome thought to return. For this reason proper replacement thoughts are necessary to complete the cycle.

Replacement thoughts can be focused on topics which

are unrelated to the troubling ones. Sue, who worried constantly about contracting cancer, could interrupt her carcenogenic thinking and substitute images of a sun-drenched beach in Southern California. However, the most effective replacement thoughts are those which deliver a more rational and realistic assessment of the problem at hand. Shifting logic is more helpful than switching topics.

For Christians, this replacement step should involve straightening out their thinking about God as well as about their world. In this chapter we have already reviewed God's interest in our distress and His desire to share in our crises. Realization of His presence and comfort is very encouraging and offers tremendous stress-reduction benefits. This realistic appraisal of God's role in our lives provides excellent replacement thoughts. After terminating our stressful thinking, we need to remind ourselves of God's love and His active involvement in our lives.

The other aspect of thought replacement concerns the irrationality of the ideas that are creating turmoil. Anxious thoughts are usually frought with illogic. We may remind ourselves repeatedly of a social faux pas resulting in significant anxiety and perceptions of ourselves as social lepers. Our stress-producing self-statements, "I'm such an idiot for calling Bob by the wrong name—I can't believe I did that; he'll never want to spend any time with me again," are usually gross exaggerations. After interrupting this personal denouncement, a more realistic replacement thought might be, "I need to apologize to Bob and use this embarrassment to help me concentrate more fully when talking to others." In this more realistic appraisal, we have not denied the incident, but rather we have reframed it in much less stressful terms. An in-depth treatment of changing our internal monologues is provided in chapter 6.

Returning to Sue, we are now ready to offer her a thought-stopping strategy to reduce her anxiety. Her first task is to detect her stressful thoughts. The obvious gremlin here is her overconcern about physical health. Working backward from her anxiety to her thoughts, she discovers that the most intense stress is accompanied by worry over the fate of her children should she die of cancer. She now must concentrate on her concerns to understand them fully. Sue recognizes the fearfulness precipitated by a bodily ache, by reflection on cancer in her family tree, or by the image of her children motherless.

Now she must plan to interrupt this thinking each time it occurs. She locates her rubber band, delivers the sting, and gives the covert command to stop.

Replacement thoughts first center on God's presence: "I must accept God's invitation to cast my cares on Him and believe that all things do work together for good in His eternal purpose. He knows the needs of my children and He loves them even more than I do." Other substitutes take a realistic perspective. "The doctor assured me that the cancer is gone. Everyone has aches and pains at times. My immediate relatives are in good health and I have no reason to believe I've inherited cancerous genes. I must focus on my life and quit thinking about death." Sue will probably need to go through this cycle many times, but she now has a strategy to beat the anxiety.

The House Won't Sell
My most recent bout with stressful thinking was occasioned by a change of residence. In 1988, I decided to return to Atlanta to enter a private practice, leaving my professorship in Indiana. The details of the new job were ironed out rapidly, and my whole family was excited to move back down south. Things seemed to be progressing nicely until suddenly there was a fly in the ointment—our house. We loved it and everyone else said it was fantastic, but no one seemed interested in buying it. As several months passed with no takers in sight, I became anxious about the prospects of carrying a financial albatross around my neck and began thinking fatalistically. "Maybe the house will never sell. I guess it's not as appealing as I thought it would be. I'll be stuck with a huge debt for twenty-five more years."

These thoughts sapped a lot of energy. I found myself repeating them continually, and this served only to deflate my motivation to spend time with my family and complete my work. Instead, I seemed to devote myself to the task of becoming the ultimate pessimist. When I finally realized how anxious I had become, I knew that something must be done. I preferred the solution of a cash buyer appearing at my door, begging me to sell the house. God had other ideas. The situation called for some serious thought-stopping.

My first task was to detect my stressful thinking. It would be simple to think that the source of the stress was purely financial. Who can afford to make house payments for an empty dwelling in another state? But this was not the big issue. I talked it out with my empathetic wife one night and discovered the real bugaboo—I hate to be out of control. The thing that really escalated my stress level was the irritation and helpless feeling that arose from my inability to control something important to me. I was used to being in charge and quickly solving my problems. I didn't adjust well to this stubborn stressor.

My next task, investigation of my thinking, was enlightening. I discovered statements like, "This house will never sell. It was foolish to make such an expensive purchase. I wish I'd never seen this place. I'll never put myself in this position again." I really knew how to sing the blues.

I found thought-interruption to be the easiest part of the process. I became very proficient at detecting the insidious ideas and at wrist-popping. At first I felt embarrassed to sport my crude rubber bracelet since some of my clients, who themselves were dealing with stressful thinking, would gather that their psychologist was having to take his own medicine. But I reasoned that stress is part of the human condition and psychologists are not immune from anxiety.

My replacement thoughts were realistic assessments of God's concern and environmental events. They went something like this: "Now stop your worrying. God recognizes your needs and has every intention of meeting them. Right now the lesson of patience is probably the reason for this trying of your faith. Besides, houses don't sell overnight in small Indiana towns. People are still coming to see the house, and eventually one will show interest. You already know two people who want to rent it if it doesn't sell."

I won't suggest that my thought-stopping was easy. Apparently, I had learned to like my stressful thinking and was really attached to it. My more rational thoughts were not nearly as inviting. I found myself having to pop, stop, and replace much more frequently than I expected—sometimes twice in a minute. But it was effective!

Personal Application
As you consider the thought-stopping technique, remember that all of us suffer from stressful thinking from time to time. These thoughts must be addressed because they trigger the physical and emotional stress response each time we entertain them. Obsessive thoughts imprison our reasoning, reduce our control, and limit our ministry effectiveness. God is intimately interested in our lives and warns us to refrain from obsessive worry. He invites and even commands us to share our burdens with Him and to accept His eternal perspective. Thought-stopping can help us eliminate the worry and can free us to accept His comfort and encouragement.

When utilizing the thought-stopping strategy, keep these pointers in mind:

● When detecting your stressful thinking, go beyond the surface to discover the real crux of the anxiety. "I don't like my job" is probably too general. "I fear I can't operate the new computer and that means I'm a failure" is more on target.

● If you can't easily pinpoint your stressful thoughts, look for clues by investigating the onset of the anxiety, or work backward from your anxiety to the most immediate thought that preceded it, looking for common themes.

● Consider your stressful thoughts thoroughly and determine every aspect of your negative thinking. Learn any disguises your anxious thoughts use to break through your barriers.

• Interrupt your negative thinking as soon as you detect it with the pop-and-stop strategy.

• Develop realistic replacement thoughts that acknowledge God's concern and that correct your illogical thinking.

• Incorporate the replacement thoughts immediately after interrupting the worrisome thinking. Don't try to rely on thought-termination alone to eliminate your anxiety.

• Plan on plenty of repetition. Obsessions and worries are very persistent and usually require countless interruptions and replacements. Don't be surprised if you have to use the technique several times in a matter of minutes.

Now you're ready to eradicate your stressful thinking. Keep your guard up and don't let your anxious thoughts off the hook!

FOUR

*"Who of you by worrying can add
a single hour to his life?"
Matthew 6:27*

Get Inoculated

Picture yourself in a contoured chair, tilted back slightly,
legs raised comfortably. Soothing music is playing in the
background. A man enters the room and makes pleasant
conversation as he looks over some papers. He then walks
to your chair, looks at you reassuringly, and turns on a
bright light above your head. He asks you to open your
mouth widely and then begins to pick at your teeth with a
shiny steel instrument. If you just gripped the arms of your
imaginary chair tightly and your knees braced, you have a
stress reaction similar to what many people feel when vis-
iting the dentist. This is an anxiety-producing situation
which most of us choose to face because of the painful
future consequences of avoidance.

The most effective way to deal with any isolated stressor
is to eliminate it. If a thorn is in your finger, you will be
better served by pulling it out than by engaging in a relaxation procedure or diverting your attention to more positive events.

However, the complexity of life often prohibits stressor
elimination or avoidance. For instance, if your job has negative components, you might choose to eliminate the stress
by quitting. But the financial consequences of termination
could be much more unpleasant than enduring the job

tasks. Perhaps the behavior of your children is stressful at times. You could eliminate this anxiety by avoiding them, but this would, of course, cause even more problems.

Most of us are confronted with anxiety-producing situations which we cannot avoid or for which the price of avoidance is very high. Since we can't eliminate these stressors, we need to develop appropriate strategies to minimize their harmful effects. We need an inoculation! The anxiety-reduction technique described in this chapter is designed specifically for coping with these unremovable stressors.

Stress Inoculation

Psychologists Donald Meichenbaum and Roy Cameron devised the stress-inoculation procedure as a psychological approach to control anxiety. They found that when under stress, we often focus on the anxiety it produces and this just makes us more nervous. It is much more beneficial to focus on the problem at hand so that we may discover the best way to solve it and reduce this anxiety. Stress inoculation is designed for this very thing. It gives us a strategy to acknowledge our feelings but allows us to devote our energies to resolution of the problem that confronts us. This practice immunizes us against the more serious effects of stress and anxiety.

We human beings are constantly talking—if not to others, then to ourselves. Our internal self-talk consists of directions which guide our actions and influence our feelings. We are most aware of these self-instructions when we are learning to perform a new task. Do you remember when you were learning to ride a bicycle? You probably instructed yourself moment by moment on the correct riding technique. Maybe your thinking went something like this: "I know I can ride this bike. I've learned everything I need to know to get started. Now let's see, I need to start with the right pedal up so I can get a good take-off. Okay, let's do it. Here I go. . . . Oh, no, I'm falling to the left. Let's see, I'll turn the front wheel left. Oh, good, I made it! Now

I'm falling to the right. Turn it to the right. Oh, good! Remember to keep pedaling. Now I've got to stop; let's see, I depress these brakes that are on the handlebar." If you are a bike-rider, you may recognize some of these self-statements. However, if you were to get on a bike today, having been used to riding one for a number of years, you probably would not state these same instructions verbally. Following them has become an automatic response.

These instructions would he marvelous if our programming were appropriate. But what if our programming were dysfunctional? What if we had learned to turn the handlebars the wrong way when we were falling and we continued to fall? We might feel hopeless that we would ever learn to ride the bike.

We instruct ourselves in all our life experiences, including our reactions to unpleasant situations. If we have learned effective management strategies, we instruct ourselves well and cope successfully with the tasks at hand. However, if we provide faulty instructions to ourselves, faulty performance follows. Sadly, dysfunctional self-statements perpetuate themselves and become automatic just like our bike-riding directions. It is as if we turn on a negative tape each time we encounter the stressor, and we follow the steps precisely. This results in poor coping.

When we routinely handle a situation poorly, we lose self-confidence and begin to feel helpless. Because we become anxious when the stressor is present, we try to stay as far from it as possible. The costs are often high since this avoidance can severely limit our freedom. When we can't avoid the stressor, we feel doomed and experience chronic stress. We focus on our anxiety and our physical discomfort. We worry about our fast heart rate, accelerated breathing, muscle tension, and perspiration, instead of concentrating on the task at hand. This does not solve the problem but only makes us more aware of our anxiety. Instead of giving ourselves instructions for dealing with the problem, we are thinking, "Oh, no! I'm really messing up now. I'm going to lose my cool. I'll never get this right.

Everyone can see that I'm a nervous wreck."

I once observed a young girl on her first visit to the roller-skating rink. Her father was standing by the rail instructing her on the proper method to maintain her balance and propel herself forward. She listened intently, repeated his instructions, but held steadfastly to the rail. Her father coaxed her, but to no avail. Soon she began telling her father her self-instructions: "I can't let go because I'm afraid I'll fall. Other people are watching, and I'll be embarrassed. I may hurt myself because this floor is hard. I don't think I'm ready. I want to go home." Her father offered all the encouragement he could muster, but he could not dissuade his daughter. She would focus only on her anxiety and, therefore, she never left the safety of the rail. They left the rink together, quite frustrated.

Jesus warned that worrying was an uneconomical use of energy and accomplishes nothing. He used the carefree birds and flowers to illustrate the futility of focusing on anxiety. He asked, "Who of you by worrying can add a single hour to his life?" (Matthew 6:27) Worrying is an unworthy use of time that we would do well to avoid.

How Stress Inoculation Works

The stress-inoculation procedure neutralizes negative self-instructions by replacing them with more functional ones. When we are able to focus on the task at hand instead of on our personal anxiety, we become more successful. These more functional self-statements accomplish three purposes:

1. They provide a means of directly lowering our anxiety.

2. They direct attention to the relevant elements of the task at hand so that we may make positive coping responses.

3. They provide a structure in which we can endorse ourselves for our success.

For many people, merely having a game plan to follow when facing known stressors adds a measure of comfort. It also engenders self-confidence and bolsters motivation to enter the previously feared arena. The four steps of the stress inoculation procedure correspond to the acronym P-A-R-T.

• Prepare. The first step is to make extensive preparation to cope with the expected negative event. This may seem rather obvious, but it is often disregarded when stressors are anticipated. People are prone either to focus on their anxiety and escalate it, or to put the situation completely out of their minds in an effort to avoid the dreadful anxiety. Both rob them of valuable preliminary time to brace for the stressor.

This preparation has two components: planning your coping strategy and preparing yourself mentally to follow the stress inoculation procedure. Let's say that your boss has asked to see you just after lunch to discuss a revenue decline in your area of the company. Your preparation may include gathering documentation for operations in your area, noting factors which influenced production, consulting with department workers, and reminding yourself that you'll use stress inoculation to help you cope. Self-statements may include: "I have all my facts together. There's really nothing to worry about because I've kept my boss informed regularly on our progress this quarter. I know exactly what to do. I have a strategy for handling this meeting. I just have to go through the steps I've practiced repeatedly. I've prayed about it; now I just have to do it."

• Acknowledge the anxious cues. Soon after encountering the stressful situation, you will probably notice some physiological arousal and anxiety building up inside of you. This is natural and to be expected. Instead of trying to ignore the anxiety, acknowledge it as your ally. You must change the meaning of this anxiety from an unwelcomed foe that will ruin your afternoon to an ally telling you it's time to practice the coping responses for which you've prepared. Do not focus on the anxiety and escalate it in your mind. Merely recognize it as a cue to begin using your stress management techniques and be ready to move on to the next step in the stress inoculation procedure.

During your meeting with the boss, your self-instructions at this step may include: "I'm getting a little anxious, but I expected that. It's nothing to worry about. It's just a signal for me to get on with the coping process. Okay, what's the next step?"

• Relaxation. Now it's time to reduce your stress by relaxing your body and mind to the greatest extent possible. Relaxation is not the natural response in a pressure situation and is available to you only through your self-instructions. Since you do not ordinarily spend a lot of time in a very stressful situation, breathing techniques are typically the most effective to use in stress inoculation. They require little time to implement, work quickly, and are not noticeable by others.

When coming to this step in your meeting with the boss, you may instruct yourself, "It's time to relax and reduce this tension. I'll just focus on my breathing and slow it down. There's no need to panic; I can slow my breathing easily without anyone even noticing what I'm doing. I'll just breathe in and out slowly.... There, it's working. I feel better already. Time to get on with the presentation."

• Task-focusing. You're in the middle of the storm, but instead of being nervous or jittery, you are composed and have a clear mind. Now it is time to instruct yourself in the most promising plan of action to handle the stressor. You've kept your head together, now use it. Follow the strategy you outlined before going into the stressful situation in a step-by-step fashion with your mind fully on the task at hand. Just as when you were learning to ride a bicycle, tell yourself each move you should make in specific terms.

Your boss is waiting for your assessment of the department, and you're ready to present your thoughts. Your self-statements may include: "Just keep my mind on the task at hand. I'll just follow the outline I put together this morning. Let's see, the first thing I need to discuss is the market fluctuations in light of the new law on imports from

overseas. . . . (After completing the presentation) There, I
did it just as planned. I kept my composure. Who could
expect any more? Thank You, Lord, for Your guidance and
comfort."

Always end your task-focusing statements with a positive pronouncement concerning your performance. It may
seem trite as you read this, but after dealing successfully
with a stressor, your personal congratulatory statements
and offers of thanksgiving to God are very helpful in building confidence in your ability to cope. The next time you
face a similar stressor, you will feel more in control of the
situation and more personally encouraged.

Randy's Dilemma

Randy was a college freshman when he entered psychotherapy with me. His presenting problem was test anxiety.
He was a very capable student with good intellectual resources and a warm personal presence—but classroom
tests left him a nervous wreck. Randy studied thoroughly
for his exams and could recite the information he was to
learn without hesitation while in my office. However, when
the professor told the class to put their books away and
ready themselves for the test, Randy became terrified. He
reported that his mind went blank and his nervousness
soared.

As I worked with Randy, I discovered that he was not a
perfectionist, nor did he feel much pressure from others to
do exceptionally well in school. His parents were very accepting of him, and his professors treated him reasonably.
It was Randy himself who was the culprit. I soon discovered from Randy that he focused on his anxiety so exclusively during a test that other thoughts were not readily
available to him. He needed some functional self-instructions to help him demonstrate his knowledge on examinations. His treatment was stress inoculation. The following
were his self-statements in the four-step procedure.

● Prepare. "I have a plan to deal with this. Old Dr. Smith
hasn't caught me off guard this time. I've read all the mate-

rial and studied the notes. I know this stuff backward and forward. I'm ready to show him my stuff. I'll just take it one step at a time. Remember, no negative self-talk."

• Acknowledge the anxious cues. "Okay, now I have the test paper. You know I'm a little bit nervous now, but I'm sure everyone else is too. Dr. Aycock said most people are a little antsy when they take a test. That's just normal. But I've got a jump on it because I can recognize it early. Anyway, a little bit of anxiety is a good thing. This is my signal to use the coping skills I've learned. I can't eliminate all the stress, but I can use it to my advantage. Everything is going just as planned. Now let's get on with it."

• Relaxation. "I've learned how to relax at will. I've eased away this kind of tension plenty of times before. I'll just control my breathing and breathe away the nervousness. Then inhale deeply. Now hold it for a few seconds.... There, I feel more relaxed already. I can focus on my breathing at any time during the hour so there's nothing to worry about."

• Task-focusing. "Just keep my mind on these questions. Take one item at a time. Now what's this first question asking? Which options can I eliminate? There's no hurry. I have plenty of time. Now go on to question two.... (After finishing test). Hey, that went well. Thank You, Lord. I didn't get every question right, but I sure got most of them. That wasn't half as bad as I expected. I knew just what I was doing the whole time."

Randy became successful in his test-taking as he followed the stress inoculation procedure on every exam. A few months later he told me that he wasn't really following the procedures anymore when he took his tests. He said that he just sort of forgot about the strategy, and it didn't seem necessary anymore. He was continuing to do well on his tests, and he didn't notice any undue anxiety during the examinations. By this I knew that Randy had incorporated these self-instructions into his thinking, and that the directions were now automatic. He didn't even recognize their existence anymore, but he followed them explicitly when taking his exams. Stress inoculation had immunized Randy to a powerful stressor in his life. He still had to study for his exams and he never really enjoyed test-taking, but now he was free to perform without anxiety.

Personal Stress Inoculation

As you consider the stress inoculation procedure for your personal use, several considerations are important. This treatment is for coping with stressful situations which you cannot eliminate or for which elimination has a high price tag. The procedure will also work when applied to removable stressors, but it certainly is not the most efficient method for dealing with them. There is no need to use a cobweb cleaner continually when you can kill the spider just as easily. So before going any further, take time to evaluate whether the situation which produces anxiety for you is directly modifiable or if it demands your adjustment to it instead.

Begin by exterminating all the unnecessary "spiders" which produce anxiety in your life. Maybe your anxiety-producing spider is a busy daily schedule that leaves no room for the inevitable interferences you encounter. This is usually modifiable through time management strategies (see chapter 7). Perhaps your practice of taking on too many obligations is spinning a web around you. Learning to say no will typically eradicate this spider for you (see chapter 11). Even minor adjustments such as putting a "No Smoking" sign in your office and removing all ashtrays or taking a less congested, albeit longer, route to work each day may be all you need to eliminate many frustrations.

When extermination is impossible or impractical, cobweb cleaning is the next best alternative. Many unremovable stressors are interpersonal in nature. It may be difficult for you to speak in front of others or deal directly with a boss or supervisor. You may cringe when you must interact with certain difficult family members or make conversation with a stranger. Perhaps you have a chronic health problem which defies medical treatment. In such cases, where anxiety is inevitable, stress inoculation may be the most effective strategy available to reduce your nervousness and keep you on track while you deal with the situation.

It is also important to remember that although stress inoculation provides you with an army of resources to cope with a stressful situation, you must provide a specific battle plan. The sequencing of your preparation, acknowledgment, and relaxation will not produce victory unless your task-focusing directions are effective. Therefore, it is imperative that you possess the appropriate skills to handle the stressor. If you don't know how to take multiple-choice examinations or how to make a coherent presentation to your boss when no anxiety is present, stress inoculation will not magically provide you with these required self-instructions. When you recognize personal deficits in the specific task-related skills needed to deal with a situation, you must learn these strategies before turning to stress inoculation.

Your Stress-Inoculation Checklist
Once you've determined that a situation is appropriate for stress inoculation, use the following questions as guidelines to generate effective self-statements. Anxiety associated with delivering a devotional is used as the example to illustrate each point.

• Preparation stage

Do your statements suggest responses which you may make *before* the stressor is encountered? (e.g., "I've prayed about this devotional and I've studied the passage extensively.")

Are your statements specific? (e.g., "I'll read directly from the outline in front of me.")

Are your sentences stated in positive terms? (e.g., "I can handle this devotional.")

Do your statements engender confidence in your skills? (e.g., "I can speak in front of a group. I've done it before.")

Do your statements remind you of the stress-inoculation

procedure itself? (e.g., "I have a game plan for dealing with any anxiety that may arise.")

- Acknowledgment stage

Is there mention of expected anxiety? (e.g., "I may become nervous. Most people do.")

Is there recognition of anxiety as it arises? (e.g., "I feel myself getting a little tense.")

Is there a reframing of anxiety from a negative to a positive light? (e.g., "I expected this anxiety. Things are going as planned.")

Is anxiety identified as an ally, signal, cue, etc.? (e.g., "I'll use this as a cue to keep me on track.")

Do your statements encourage you to continue the procedure? (e.g., "It's time to go on to my relaxation.")

- Relaxation stage

Are the anxiety-reducing effects of relaxation stated? (e.g., "I know I can reduce this anxiety by relaxing.")

Is a specific relaxation procedure detailed? (e.g., "Now slow that breathing down.")

Are the positive effects of your relaxation acknowledged? (e.g., "It's working. I'm already feeling less tense.")

- Task-focusing stage

(These statements will vary with the anxiety situation you are facing, but several guidelines are still in order.)

Are the skills pertinent to the task at hand? (e.g., "I'll just open with the story I prepared.")

Are your statements phrased in *action* terms? (e.g., "Now I'll read the Scripture passage I've selected.")

Are your directions specific? (e.g., "I'll stop at verse 8.")

When stepwise skills are necessary, is there a statement describing the action to be taken at each step in the sequence? (e.g., "I've finished reading the verses; now I'll ask for group responses.")

Are reasonable alternatives identified in situations which may demand various responses? (e.g., "If no one responds, I'll offer the observations I wrote on my outline.")

Do you congratulate yourself for your coping efforts? (e.g., "Hey, I did a good job.")

Do you give thanks to God for His assistance? (e.g., "Thank You, Lord, for Your comfort.")

Do you suggest future success in your statements? (e.g., "That wasn't so bad. I could do that again.")

When you can answer yes to all of these questions, you're ready to begin confronting those unpleasant situations which cannot reasonably be avoided. The self-statements may seem cumbersome initially, but any new skill we learn demands attention to detail. Just like riding a bike, the instructions become automatic over time as we use them successfully. Now you have a strategy to combat life's dreaded events. You can remain calm and stick to your plan of attack. You've been inoculated!

SECTION 2

Our thoughts exert a tremendous influence on our feelings and actions. Our inability to think creatively, change negative thinking, or plan our lives causes us many problems. It is tragic when we fail to harness the vast capabilities of our thinking to insure optimal health. Indeed, the power of our minds is a terrible resource to waste.

Paul admonished Christians to have the same mind as Jesus Christ. Jesus was always in control of His thinking. He resisted human interpretations of events in favor of taking God's perspective. Jesus remained single-minded in His devotion to His Father and acted consistently with God's will and plan for His life. He thought both logically and lovingly even when His circumstances seemed chaotic and those around Him were treacherous. Jesus was always aware of His primary life goal and never allowed temporal problems to divert Him from His purpose.

The three chapters in Section 2 describe strategies for improving our thinking. We often struggle unnecessarily with problems because we fail to gain a proper perspective of them and persist fruitlessly in ineffective actions destined for repeated failure. Chapter 5 looks at creative problem-solving and offers strategies to challenge our limiting assumptions, unbind our thinking, and generate new solutions to problems.

In chapter 6 we examine the role our thoughts play in determining feelings and behaviors, along with strategies for detecting irrational and unhelpful thinking. Methods effective in modifying unhealthy thinking are detailed with an emphasis on developing a biblical point of view.

Chapter 7 also contains techniques useful in setting goals and managing our time. The major theme is to plan our work and work our plan. Strategies for structuring our lives are included as well.

FIVE

*"It is not good to have zeal without
knowledge, nor to be hasty and miss
the way."*
Proverbs 19:2

Solve Your Problems

Although human problems come in many shapes and sizes, they all arise from deviations between how things are and how we think they should be. Our expectations actually determine the number and severity of the problems we encounter. If we have no expectations, we have no problems. Failing to receive a paycheck for work you've completed is only a problem if you expect to be paid. Finding ten baskets of dirty laundry in front of your washing machine is not a problem if you run a laundry cleaning business.

Interpersonal problems boil down to differences in expectations as well. An individual with lower expectations will have difficulty understanding the gravity of a problem defined by a person with higher expectations. For example, college roommates often disagree on the organization of their dormitory room. An individual reared in a family which placed a premium on organization and cleanliness has been reinforced for the practice of orderly room maintenance. These behaviors have become normative for this student. Her expectation is that personal belongings should be organized properly and put away. A roommate who has a different developmental history may hold the expectation that her room should be comfortable, and that articles most naturally belong where they were last placed. Finding the room in a disorganized condition would be problematic to one roommate and irrelevant to the other.

In their delightful book *Change* (New York: W.W. Norton and Company, 1974), Paul Watzlawick, John Weakland, and Richard Fisch draw a distinction between a *problem* and a *difficulty*. They suggest that problems are resolvable whereas difficulties must simply be tolerated. When we fail to make this distinction, we transform difficulties into problems and create unnecessary suffering. As Bishop Berkeley said, "We first raise the dust and then complain we cannot see." Christians sometimes go through periods in which they experience little spiritual growth and find devotions and prayer to be taxing. When a believer interprets this stagnation as evidence that he is not truly justified, he may embark on a discouraging journey of self-doubt and repeatedly attempt to gain *real* salvation. Seasoned Christians realize that spiritual growth comes in spurts and that plateaus and distractions are part of the human condition. Failure to recognize this growth pattern converts it into a problem of eternal proportions.

Determining if a problem does or doesn't exist is the first critical step in the problem-solving process. There's no pressing need to locate the flashlight if the electricity is coming back on in two minutes. Allotting time to decide if and when to take action is a wise precaution. We often need to pray along with St. Francis of Assisi, "Lord, give me the serenity to accept those things which cannot be changed, the courage to change those things which can and should be changed, and the wisdom to know the difference."

Defining the Problem
Once a problem has been identified, the effective problem-solver will take ample time to understand it fully and define it precisely. Sometimes this is easy. When he drops a brick on his foot, his problem definition is all too evident! Indeed, the majority of problems we face have clear defini-

tions. Tired eyes mean we need sleep; a fuel gauge on empty indicates a problem resolvable at the next gas station. We may not even think of these as problems because we regularly encounter them.

The problem for which there is no obvious solution is the one which demands considerable attention. Sometimes the problem is clear, but the possible solutions are confusing. Such is the case for the new college graduate who recognizes her problem (needing a job to sustain herself) but finds a whole range of solutions. At other times it is hard to put a finger on the problem itself. Most of us have had a feeling of uncomfortability with no clear indication why we felt that way. A good place to begin the definition process is by analyzing our expectations.

When we recognize a problem in our spiritual lives, we should consider our expectations. Perhaps we feel unspiritual because an evil thought crosses our minds or a prayer isn't answered exactly as we had planned. The problem can be defined as disappointed expectations about our personal control of our thought life or about God's response to our request. We can now attack the problem.

When an interpersonal problem arises, it is necessary to learn the expectations of all persons involved for a proper definition of the problem. Marriage counselors face this task routinely as spouses often hold very different expectations, sometimes without bothering to tell each other what they want. Once I saw a couple in marriage counseling who had a major fight over the position of the toilet seat. She thought it should always be left down, and he had a habit of leaving it up. The real issue underlying the toilet seat position was respect. She felt unappreciated because her husband didn't take the time and effort to perform a simple nicety for her. He interpreted his failing as trivial and her hysteria over it as a symptom of insanity. A common definition of the problem in terms of respect made a solution possible.

Sometimes we define our problems too narrowly, limiting our thinking severely. A student becomes depressed because she is not accepted into the sorority she pledged. She defines her problem as assured unhappiness in college because of this rejection. A fuller investigation of her predicament uncovers some important issues. She is seeking social enhancement and views sorority membership as a means of gaining instant camaraderie with the sorority sisters and guaranteed attention from the males on campus. Being rejected for membership in the sorority is not the real problem. Instead, an inability to connect socially with other students is her main concern. Gaining acceptance into the sorority may not be attainable, but enhancing social contacts lies well within her reach if she learns appropriate social skills and places herself visibly in the social arena. This new definition of her problem makes it easier to resolve. The same is often true for us as we define our problems in the broadest terms.

We must also be careful not to confuse a problem with its symptoms. A concerned parent may bring twelve-year-old Johnny to the psychologist complaining that he seems depressed, is doing poorly in school, argues constantly with his sister, and will not observe household regulations. The psychologist could develop a treatment plan for Johnny which includes medication to relieve depression, a tutor for assistance at school, communication training for Johnny and his sister to reduce arguments, and a reward system for obeying the rules of the house. However, a competent psychologist would inquire about the events surrounding the onset of these problems. Suppose she discovered that these misbehaviors arose when Johnny's father took a traveling sales position six months ago. The problem would probably be defined in terms of Johnny's uncomfortability with the absence of his father and uncertainty about his father's continued love for him. Family therapy focusing on relationship issues would hold much more promise than the individual symptom prescriptions offered above.

These definition skills require us to step back from our circumstances in order to gain perspective. Some people like to visualize their problems in different life situations or reduce them to numbers which can be more logically manipulated. It is always encouraging to define problems in terms of a personal deficit because the flip side can easily become our goal. It is hard to attack a problem defined fuzzily like, "My children are turning out wrong." It is much better to state the problem, "I have not discovered the appropriate discipline techniques to use with my children." The latter is easily be transformed into a goal which is attackable.

Seeking Information

After a problem is defined, our search for a proper solution can get underway. A key step is gathering the right amount of relevant information. Too much or too little information may actually impede the process of problem-solving. All of us have had the unfortunate experience of being waited on by a salesperson who told us much more than we wanted to know about a product or an equally frustrating encounter with a novice who knew nothing about his wares. My personal experiences with the computer yield numerous cases of information overload. It seems that the magical machine is extremely literal and refuses to supply me with anything if I deviate in the slightest from its expected mode of input. And when the statistical program does run, the voluminous output sheets present so much data that wading through them is a discouraging task.

Information is available to us from a vast array of sources including people, the electronic media, and the printed page. However, it's amazing how often we fail to utilize these resources. How often have you wandered fruitlessly through the supermarket looking for an item instead of asking the grocer for its aisle location? Unwillingness to ask for help or consult information sources results in a tremendous amount of lost time and unresolved problems. Don't be afraid to benefit from the experiences of others.

One resource we cannot afford to ignore is the Bible. Problem resolution which fails to take God's eternal perspective into focus leads us into further difficulties. In 2 Samuel 6, the account of David's delivery of the ark from Baalah back to Jerusalem is detailed. Even though Moses gave strict instructions that the ark was to be carried on poles, David set the ark on a new cart drawn by oxen. When an ox stumbled, Uzzah reached out to steady the ark and was struck dead for his seemingly benevolent action. The failure to follow pertinent information from the Scriptures resulted in serious problems for these Israelites.

The Bible speaks to many problems that we encounter. Indeed, replacement behaviors are often prescribed along with prohibitions of misbehaviors. For example, in Ephesians 4:28 we read, "He who has been stealing must steal no longer, but must work, doing something useful with his own hands, that he may have something to share with those in need." At other times specific answers to problems aren't given but a principle is implied.

Challenging Limiting Assumptions

Once a New Yorker who desired to return to London to see his family pooled all of his resources and booked passage on a ship bound for England. The man soon became famished, but he dared not enter the ship's dining room since he didn't have a penny to his name. After the first full week at sea, he could stand the hunger no longer and made his way to the captain's galley to plead for a morsel of sustenance. The captain received the desperate man and listened intently to his description of hunger and his proposals to perform chores in exchange for nourishment. The captain immediately ordered food to be brought and informed his weakened guest, "The cost of your ticket to board my vessel entitled you to three meals a day in our dining room. You had only to present yourself at the door, and you would have been granted entrance."

Like this forlorn passenger, very often we entrap ourselves in seemingly hopeless situations because we make inaccurate assumptions and never bother to check them out. We induce paralysis routinely with the words "can't" and "won't." We may say to ourselves, "I can't sing well enough to join the choir" and listen enviously each Sunday wishing we too could perform. A teenager may say, "Donna won't ever go out with me" and sit at home Saturday night while across town Donna does the same. These limiting assumptions imprison our thinking and significantly hamper problem resolution.

To test your thinking flexibility, try the following problems:

• Consider the nine dots in figure 1. Draw four straight lines without lifting your pencil from the paper in such a way as to connect all nine dots.

• Discover the familiar phrases represented by the arrangements of words and symbols in figure 2.

If you're still puzzled, the solutions to these problems appear at the end of this chapter.

In order to solve these problems, you had to challenge limiting assumptions. In solving the nine dot problem, you likely assumed that you had to stay within the square. Failure to figure out the phrases was probably caused by a literal reading of the words and a disregard for the arrangements of letters. Now that you have disposed of your limiting assumptions, the solutions seem so simple, just like the surprise endings on "Alfred Hitchcock Presents" that bring the whole story into focus. Indeed, many of our problems have more simplistic solutions than we usually imagine.

The Bible is filled with examples which dispel limiting assumptions. Jesus frequently introduced paradoxes into His teachings such as, "Whoever tries to keep his life will lose it, and whoever loses his life will preserve it" (Luke 17:33) or "The greatest among you will be your servant" (Matthew 23:11). He vividly illustrated this paradox to his disciples when He undertook the ultimate servitude and washed their feet.

Robert Kennedy's famous quote, "Some men look at the world and ask 'Why?' I look at the world and ask 'Why not?'" should express our approach to problems. We should ask ourselves, "Why *not* give our child a choice in

Figure 1

●   ●   ●

●   ●   ●

●   ●   ●

Figure 2

a. $\begin{bmatrix} \text{INCOME} \\ \\ \\ \end{bmatrix}$

b. O
    V
    A
    T
    I
    O
    N

c. sitting
    world

d. N I N T H

her discipline?" "Why *not* approach our neighbor about his relationship to God?" "Why *not* support that missionary venture?" We must liberate our imprisoned thinking!

Seeking a Wide Range of Alternatives

What parent hasn't heard, "Dad, there's *nothing* to do!" When my daughters offer this complaint to me, I do what most parents do—run through the list of activities available. "You can ride your bike, color some pictures, read a book, watch a videotape, play with the neighbor, or read ahead in your schoolwork. You've got lots of toys in the playroom. You can play with your sister or give Mom a hand around the house." Those last two suggestions guarantee their retreat.

Children are shortsighted and have difficulty occupying themselves with any one of a myriad of activities that are at their fingertips. Most adults simply can't find the time to engage in even half of the things we want to do. But when it comes to problem-solving, adults are often just as shortsighted as their myopic children. We fail to actively seek a full range of solutions which may be available to us, and thus create inactivity, discouragement, and unsatisfying resolutions to our problems.

Our unwillingness to identify a wide range of options is not usually a consequence of our inability to generate alternatives, but is rather due to our lack of tolerance for the ambiguity which is present until a choice is made. Over fifty years ago the German Gestalt psychologists demonstrated our need for closure to terminate the tension which accompanies incompleteness.[1] I'm amazed at the frequency with which some people will make a choice—any choice—just to dispense with a matter. This may work fine in a fast food line, but it does not work well when buying a car or deciding on prospective employees.

Management consultant Herbert Simon describes these different levels of sophistication at which problems are solved or decisions are made as *satisficing* versus *optimizing. Satisficing* means selecting the first alternative which meets our minimal standards. We satisfice when we select a parking place or choose a restaurant while traveling. *Optimizing* involves a much more sophisticated analysis of a problem, along with consideration of alternatives and selection of a course of action. Optimizing is usually employed when we consider a job change or select a church home. The importance of a problem should dictate which problem-solving approach to use.

Unfortunately, we sometimes choose the first alternative available to us (satisficing) instead of the best one (optimizing) in order to make the decision and move on. A hasty decision may bring a short-term release of decision anxiety but precipitates greater stress in the long run as other problems begin to emerge. I've seen many couples who made a satisficing decision to wed, to relieve their loneliness, and then regretted for many years their failure to optimize. The Book of Proverbs is replete with warnings to take the time to optimize when making important decisions. For example, Solomon advises, "It is not good to have zeal without knowledge, nor to be hasty and miss the way" (Proverbs 19:2). Consideration of the full range of alternatives in problem-solving requires patience and a tolerance for some tension.

Identifying many possible solutions to a problem requires imagination and creativity. While on the battlefield it takes little imagination to determine what to do when an enemy who as been shooting at you leaves himself open for counterattack. But should you risk your army to an enthusiastic teenager who challenges a nine-foot giant? King Saul did this when he allowed David to represent Israel in a contest with Goliath. This decision incorporated faith into the equation.

Sometimes conflicting information makes it hard to pick the best option available. Such was the case in 1962 when the Kennedy administration faced the crisis of Russian nuclear missiles being moved into Cuba. Numerous retaliatory alternatives were suggested by cabinet members and even on the critical day on which the Soviets agreed to dismantle this threat, conflicting information was received at the White House. Early in the day a conciliatory message came from Premier Khrushchev offering to retreat, but later a more hostile communication arrived from the Russian leader. Most of the President's advisers believed they were back to square one in negotiations, but the Attorney General came up with an ingenious plan. The President accepted the positive message from Khrushchev, ignored the latter, and negotiated a settlement as if no discouraging message had been received.

When generating alternatives, avoid limiting assumptions which stifle creativity and restrict possibilities. Combine facts and imaginative ideas in creative ways. If nine numbers can be arranged in 362,880 ways, imagine what can be done with nine ideas!

There are a number of strategies which are very useful for increasing our option pool. One of the most common is brainstorming—the uncritical listing of all solutions which come to mind. The key to effective brainstorming is the adoption of an *uncritical attitude* so that faultfinding is suspended, and no idea is censored automatically. In fact, the silly or humorous ideas can have merit themselves and often create energy to continue the process. I find that almost all of my creative titles for manuscripts and business are generated through brainstorming. Sometimes, the sillier the session, the better the end product. *After* the brainstorming well runs dry, critical evaluation of each item is permissible, but only then.

American business if finding solutions to some of their problems by looking into the world of nature for answers. Berkeley Rice describes how this worked for potato chip manufacturers.[2] This snack food producer was concerned because their product required so much space in warehouses and on supermarket shelves. However, tighter packaging was difficult since the chips are brittle and crumble easily. Attempts to solve this dilemma were ineffective until someone suggested that dried leaves are brittle like potato chips, and are hard to pack tightly without crumbling. However, it was observed that wet leaves are capable of being tightly packed because they mold to the shape of the leaves above and below them. The answer: cut potato chips to a uniform size and shape, moisten them, and pack them tightly together. The result: Pringles and other canned chips that require relatively little storage or shelf space.

We may even be able to solve organizational problems by studying the interactions of social insects such as bees or ants or perhaps discover a means of emotional stability through the laws of physics or chemistry.

Sometimes external circumstances are not amenable to change, and we must look internally for answers to our problems. If you wish to play professional basketball but you're an uncoordinated 5'10", a change in personal expectations is probably your only avenue to resolution. Indeed, these modifications of thinking often offer the most expedient solutions to our problems because we can personally control what we say to ourselves. I find that most couples who seek me out for marriage counseling benefit from learning a few relational skills such as communication techniques; however, the lion's share of marital discord is relieved by changing each spouse's expectations and self-statements about his mate to approximate reality more closely. Likewise, frustrations on the job can often be reframed as aspects of the job itself for which we're compensated, instead of unnatural villains which we don't deserve.

Considering the Consequences

At one time starfish threatened the fishing industry because they were so prevalent on the ocean floor and regularly became entangled in fishing nets. Starfish had no commercial value and were regarded as a significant hassle to the seamen who constantly had to disengage them from their nets. To eliminate these nuisances, the fishermen would cut the starfish in several pieces and return them to the deep. What they didn't realize was that a starfish can regenerate a whole body out of any portion of itself. Because the fishermen did not understand the *consequences* of their chosen solution to the starfish problem, they were actually multiplying these sea creatures.

When we fail to consider the consequences of our alternatives fully, we invite further problems. The skills in considering consequences are logical: assessments of cost/benefits, practical limitations, feasibility, etc. The quagmires are created when we overlook the long-term effects of an option or the social implications of a choice. For you to hold five different offices in the church may be helpful in filling immediate staffing needs, but it may also require extraordinary time commitments away from your family and preclude others from ministry opportunity.

One of the most repeated lessons in the Scriptures admonishes people to gain God's spiritual perspective and weigh the temporal benefits of a decision against the eternal ones. Whether for meat in the desert or a king to rule over them, the Children of Israel constantly pleaded for things which were detrimental to them. Jesus rebuked His disciples for suggesting that He call down fire from heaven to destroy Samaritans who opposed Him, or for asking that He prevent those outside of His small band from performing mighty works in His name. We may fall into the trap of praying earnestly for something that will only bring misery.

Several decades ago many godly Alabamans prayed unceasingly for relief from the hordes of boll weevils which were destroying their cotton crops and threatening the primary industry of their state. Today the boll weevil is honored in Alabama because its devastation of the state's king cotton forced these Southerners to diversify into farming multiple crops, thus improving their economy.

It is imperative that Christians possess a working knowledge of the Scriptures to help them recognize the consequences of their choices and also to avoid unnecessary suffering. King Solomon is a case in point. He accumulated such enormous wealth that even household articles were made of gold, and silver was as common in Jerusalem as stones. He gathered a mighty military force including

12,000 horses imported from Egypt and Cicily. He even accumulated 700 wives and 300 concubines. His subjects must have applauded Solomon for his opulence that symbolized God's blessings on the nation and for his provision of superior defenses (1 Kings 10–11).

However, Israel's wisest ruler ignored God's rules about appropriate behaviors for the Jewish monarch. In Deuteronomy 17, we read specific guidelines for the actions of future kings:

> *The king, moreover, must not acquire great numbers of horses for himself or make the people return to Egypt to get more of them, for the Lord has told you, "You are not to go back that way again." He must not take many wives, or his heart will be led astray. He must not accumulate large amounts of silver and gold. (vv. 16-17)*

The king was to copy these principles by hand and read them daily to insure a long reign for himself and his descendants. Solomon's wives and material assets turned his heart from the Lord, and as a result his kingdom was divided when he died.

We must familiarize ourselves with God's principles if we are to understand fully the consequences of our choices. We must recognize God's prescriptions for interpersonal behavior—like answering gently to avoid unnecessary anger. We must understand God's economy, which places a greater emphasis on laying up spiritual treasures than on accumulating wealth. We have to see that our marital relationships can be better enhanced by each partner giving God the preeminent position and priority attention rather than directing these to our spouses. Such biblical principles often defy human logic.

Taking Action
The next step in problem-solving is to take action on the most promising alternative we've identified. But this is of-

ten where the process breaks down. We opt for inaction because it requires energy to implement something new. We may not like the way things are, but we take comfort in knowing what to expect. We are often like the guy trapped on the top floor of a burning building—he is afraid to jump into the fireman's net and so becomes very optimistic that the raging fire will somehow magically subside. Problems rarely vanish. In fact, ignoring a problem usually makes it seem much more foreboding and discourages future action. This is the wisdom offered in the suggestion immediately to remount a horse that has thrown you.

When you decide to implement your chosen alternative, you should focus fully on your strategy to resolve the problem and not on your emotional reactions which may interfere. Reduce your action plan to manageable steps which are clearly defined, so your progress can be recognized and charted. It's much more discouraging to look up and see the whole mountain you must climb than to focus merely on the next ledge you must reach. If you give yourself encouragement for advances made, you will motivate continued energy expenditure.

Analyzing Our Choices

After action is taken, there is a final step. Good problem-solvers analyze the effectiveness of their choices. This is often laborious, but the investment pays a high dividend because it guides future actions on the same or similar problems. It also instills confidence in our successes.

Our analysis can be greatly aided by inviting others to offer critiques. This compensates for our own naturally positive or negative ideas. Of course, others are only as helpful as their reactions are honest, and we will not benefit from feedback from others, or even from our own intuitive evaluations, unless we adopt an open and nondefensive posture.

Let's take the example of Ted who began teaching a high school age Sunday School class six months ago. He noticed that his students were polite but unenthusiastic, and thus decided that he wasn't reaching them effectively. Ted progressed through the problem-solving steps and implemented the alternative to change his teaching style from lecture to discussion. Now he notices more class participation, but is still unsure of his success. He may invite a seasoned high school teacher into the class or tape-record a lesson for more unintrusive observation. This will require risk-taking since Ted is putting his actions on trial.

If the feedback is honest and positive, Ted will feel validated and confident. But what if some problems are uncovered? One option is to scrap the discussion format and try the next most promising alternative. However, it may be that Ted has selected an excellent teaching style but needs to change lesson topics and develop more affirming behaviors. He may initiate lessons on relevant and interesting teen topics such as sexuality, developing one's own identity, or vocational decision-making. He may need to learn to restate students' ideas before giving his own perspective and to reinforce students for offering any opinions. In this way Ted's basic decision is affirmed, but his performance is tuned up.

Sometimes our evaluation of only marginal success in an attempted solution to a problem is accurate, but we see no other reasonable alternative actions. After insuring that we carried out our plan as well as could be expected and that amendments would not be helpful, our remaining strategy is to modify our expectations of the achievable results. Perhaps Ted discovers that he is presenting material in the most conducive manner, but class response remains lukewarm. He may need to recognize that students in this age group do not speak up, for fear of negative evaluation from their peers. He can reframe his expectations so that he is satisfied with a thorough job of presenting lesson material and then entertaining the discussion that does arise. This too qualifies as success!

Figure 3
Solution to the Nine Dot Problem

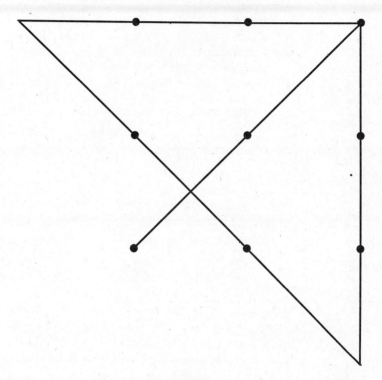

Figure 4
Solutions to the Familiar Phrase Problems

a. Upper income bracket

b. A standing ovation

c. Sitting on top of the world

d. Bottom of the ninth

"Finally, brothers, whatever is true,
whatever is noble, whatever is right,
whatever is pure, whatever is lovely,
whatever is admirable—if anything is
excellent or praiseworthy—think about
such things." Philippians 4:8

Think Again

Naaman was a successful Syrian general. He was a wealthy man, a valiant soldier, and was highly regarded by his king. But Naaman had leprosy. His search for a cure from this dreaded disease is unfolded in 2 Kings 5. Upon hearing from a servant girl about the mighty prophet in Israel, Naaman assembled treasures of silver, gold, and clothing and hand-delivered this along with a letter of request from his sovereign to the King of Israel. He expected to regain his health through his riches and his political pull. After much consternation, the desperate King of Israel sent Naaman to the Prophet Elisha, in hopes that Naaman's health could be restored and any argument with the mighty Syrian government could be averted.

When the caravan of horses, chariots, and riches arrived at Elisha's door, the prophet merely sent a messenger out to the general directing him to wash himself seven times in the Jordan River. Naaman was enraged that he had come all the way to Israel, bearing gifts, only to be snubbed by the celebrated holy man. He couldn't believe he was refused a personal audience. "I thought that he would surely come out to me and stand and call on the name of the Lord his God, wave his hand over the spot and cure me of my leprosy" (2 Kings 5:11). He was furious at the idea of dipping in the muddy Jewish river when clean waters abounded in the familiar Damascus countryside.

Fortunately for Naaman, he surrounded himself with wise servants. One of them reasoned with his master that just because the prescription was simple, albeit a little unorthodox, didn't mean it wouldn't work. He pointed out that he would do any hard task to receive the elusive cure. Why not try it? He had nothing to lose. With this new thinking in mind, Naaman took his whole body (not to mention his disappointed expectations) down under the waters of the Jordan, and after seven dips his disease vanished. Naaman's changed thinking was essential in his restortation to health and won his heart over to the Lord.

We are often like Naaman, steeped in our preconceived notions and imprisoned thinking to such an extent that our emotional leprosy spoils our happiness. The cure may not be as hard as we think, since our thinking itself is usually the key. In this chapter we will investigate the role which thinking plays in determining our emotions, and then learn strategies to improve our moods by modifying unhelpful thoughts.

The Focal Process

The idea that thoughts produce feelings is nothing new. The ancient Stoic philosopher Epictetus once stated, "Men are not disturbed by things, but by the view they take of them. When we meet with troubles, become anxious or depressed, let us never blame anyone but our opinions about things." In *Hamlet*, Shakespeare wrote, "There is nothing either good or bad, but thinking makes it so." Abraham Lincoln commented, "People are about as happy as they make up their minds to be." And in Proverbs 23:7, we read, "As a man thinketh in his heart, so is he" (KJV). While teaching His disciples about money, Jesus asserted the importance of perceptions:

> *The eye is the lamp of the body. If your eyes are good, your whole body will be full of light. But if your eyes*

are bad, your whole body will be full of darkness. If
then the light within you is darkness, how great is
that darkness! (Matthew 6:22-23)

Indeed a heavenly focus could help Paul say, "We are
hard-pressed on every side, but not crushed; perplexed, but
not in despair; persecuted, but not abandoned; struck
down, but not destroyed" (2 Corinthians 4:8-9). Negative
emotions could not get the best of Paul: his thinking provided him with a framework to understand his persecu-
tions.

Psychologists have heavily researched the thinking/
feeling relationship. For instance, one of the best-known
studies was conducted by Stanley Schacter and J.E. Singer
to demonstrate how beliefs affect feelings.[3] The researchers injected their human subjects with adrenaline, a drug
which heightens physiological arousal. Some of the participants were told what to expect from the hormone injec-
tion, while others were misinformed or told nothing at all.
The subjects were then randomly exposed to different
emotionally charged situations like answering a question-
naire which said derogatory things about their mothers or
being placed in a room with a happy-go-lucky person who
made them laugh. After this the people were tested to determine the kind and degree of emotion they experienced.
The group which knew what to expect from the adrenaline
attributed their arousal to the drug and reported little other
emotion. However, the uninformed and misinformed
groups showed much more emotion and in each case the
emotion they did report was determined by the situations
they were exposed to (whether anger or euphoria). The
study showed that when we are aroused, our internal explanations for the arousal determine our emotions. If we
don't know what generates our arousal, we look around for
any cues supplied by the environment and adopt these as
our emotions. What we say to ourselves really directs our
feelings.

Our beliefs and attitudes have a moment-to-moment impact on our lives. We are constantly involved in one-way conversations with ourselves. This personal self-talk is influenced by our beliefs about ourselves, our attitudes about the world and God, and our attitudes about ourselves in relation to the world and God. If we believe we are loved by God, we'll feel secure and accepted. If we accept the fact that many people in the world misbehave regularly, the evening news won't be as disturbing to us.

Many beliefs are so firmly entrenched that we don't even consider whether they are true or not. This may be fine if these beliefs are accurate, but it can be devastating if the beliefs are wrong. A woman who has been told very often that she is incompetent may accept this appraisal unquestioningly and feel insecure. A man who has been taught that God is unconcerned about his daily matters will feel helpless when a crisis arises which has no human solution. This is why our early training and childhood experiences are so critical and why psychotherapists devote time to these details many decades after they occur. Beliefs cannot be changed until they are understood. Consequently, negative feelings persist until we modify the beliefs which underlie them.

Thoughts and Actions
Thinking influences our behavior. If you are riding on a crowded bus quietly reading your newspaper, and someone steps on your foot, your first emotional reaction will probably be one of anger since common courtesy dictates care in handling oneself around others. When looking up to express your irritation, you notice that the offending person is wearing dark glasses and holding a dog in harness by her side. How does your reaction change? You may be more inclined to offer your seat to the blind woman than to offer commentary on her social behavior. On the other hand, if you look up and find that the foot belongs to a teenager who is as healthy as she is careless, your response might be quite different.

Our thinking affects our motivation and our ability to

obey God's laws as well. In Ephesians 4 Paul contrasts the actions of Children of the light and unbelievers. He characterizes non-Christians as being imprisoned by "the futility of their thinking," resulting in indulgence in every kind of moral impurity. He then calls for Christians to "be made new in the attitudes of (their) minds" and evidence the holy and righteous behaviors that are produced by this thinking. When nonbelievers spurn God's commands and misbehave, they are following what their mental programming calls for them to do.

It should come as no surprise that our thinking affects our choices as well. This is obvious when we are rationally working through problems and listing the strengths and weaknesses of different alternatives. Such is the case when we consider a new job or shop for a car. However, it is much less striking when we are not concentrating on a decision. This is why social prejudices are so insidious. Social psychologists have demonstrated how we show favor to persons who are our preferred color, age, or body build by our eye contact, smiles, and positive words. Most of the put-downs experienced by minorities do not come from blatant bigots, but rather from persons who would cringe at the word *racist*.

Perhaps the strongest prohibition against racism in the Scriptures was given to Peter while he lodged at the house of Cornelius, a Roman centurion. God came to Peter through a trance and clearly communicated His love and concern for all people. Peter then persuaded the entire Jewish church that God had granted salvation to the Gentiles. Yet Paul reports in Galatians 2 that Peter later practiced such blatant discrimination against the Gentiles that Paul had to confront him. Because deeply ingrained thinking is obstinate and stubbornly resists behavior change, we proceed oblivious to its poison. Anyone who wishes to overcome racial, religious, or sexual prejudice should begin by challenging his basic stereotypes of these different groups. This will be more effective than merely resolving to act in a more accepting way.

Thinking also affects health. Sick people who have no faith in medical treatment or in their ability to recover from an illness are likely to prolong their convalescence. Their thinking becomes a self-fulfilling prophecy. The same apparently holds for spiritual intervention into sickness. All three synoptic Gospels report that Jesus could do few miracles in His hometown of Nazareth because of the unbelief of the citizens. Jesus even chided His disciples for lack of faith when their efforts to heal those encountered on their journeys were unsuccessful. Straight thinking is critical to physical well-being whether help is being sought from human or divine sources.

Expectations

Uncle Remus tells the story of Brer Rabbit, who is captured by the cunning Brer Fox. He pleads with his captor to deal with him in whatever dastardly way he chooses, but to refrain from throwing him into the thistle-infested briar patch. His petitions are so impassioned that Brer Fox becomes quite convinced that flinging his adversary into the dreaded briar patch is the worst of all fates for the pesky rabbit. It is only after he executes the sentence that Brer Fox hears the rabbit laugh, "I was born and bred in the briar patch," and discovers he has been outwitted by a sly opponent.

Like Brer Fox our expectations exert a great influence over our feelings and actions. If our expectations are met regularly, we function very well. But if our expectations are disappointed, we become unhappy with our choices. This often brings couples to the marriage counseling office. When their relationship fails to meet the Hollywood standard of continual excitement and uninterrupted bliss, they are disconcerted. They never planned for the mundane aspects of married life, and now they wonder if their selection was flawed.

Many of our expectations arise from our characteristic ways of viewing the world. The optimist sees an opportunity in every problem and expects a challenge. The pessimist sees a problem in every opportunity and expects a disappointment. We seem to get what we look for. "He who seeks good finds good will, but evil comes to him who searches for it" (Proverbs 11:27). "To the pure, all things are pure, but to those who are corrupted and do not believe, nothing is pure. In fact, both their minds and consciences are corrupted" (Titus 1:15).

Thomas is a striking illustration of the power of negative expectations. Here was a man who expected the worst. He announced that Jesus' plan to return to Judea to revive the deceased Lazarus would culminate in their collective deaths. Thomas quickly resigned himself to a fatalistic attitude when Christ was crucified, and was absent from the meeting of the remaining ten disciples who were visited by the risen Lord. Thomas dismissed the claims of his comrades that Jesus was alive, and boldly asserted that only physical contact with Christ's wounds would change his expectations. Fortunately, Jesus later appeared to the doubter and erased his skepticism. Because Thomas held generally negative expectations, his name is still associated with doubt. His surname, *Didymus*, means "the twin." I wonder how often our faithless expectations make us Thomas' twin.

Expectations must be realistic to induce appropriate actions and feelings. We can modify our expectations if we are willing to question our assumptions. We do this when we are converted and transfer reliance for our well-being exclusively from ourselves to a participation with God. Expectations can change when we examine the unforeseen consequences of a challenge to our thoughts. This was the case with Thomas when he met the risen Lord and with Naaman after he reluctantly dipped in the cleansing Jordan. Expectations can die through repeated disappointments. Such was the case with the townspeople in the story of the shepherd boy who, to amuse himself, cried "Wolf." Their repeated needless attempts to rescue the lad caused the villagers to ignore the boy's genuine call for help.

Double-Mindedness

Sometimes it's not one negative thought which deflates our feeling, but rather two or more ideas which compete for our adoption or loyalty. The Bible refers to this state as double-mindedness. It is well illustrated in 1 Kings 18, when Elijah came out of hiding and challenged the prophets of Baal to a contest on Mount Carmel. Israel, languishing in a deep drought and famine, had been without a visible witness from God since Ahab and Jezebel began exterminating the Lord's prophets. Elijah diagnosed the people's problem as double-mindedness and asked, "How long will you waver between two opinions? If the Lord is God, follow Him; but if Baal is God, follow him" (v. 21). He recognized the anxiety and confusion of living with competing loyalties, and he demonstrated the Lord's superiority mightily to the people.

James describes the double-minded person as one who is unstable in every aspect of his life. He warns that effective prayer must be based in an attitude of expectant faith rather than in tenuousness. When Pharisees suggested that Jesus exorcised demons through the power of Satan, He responded by reasoning that even Beelzebub could not achieve his goals if he was not single-minded. He argued eloquently that "every kingdom divided against itself will be ruined, and every city or houshold divided against itself will not stand" (Matthew 12:25). Double-mindedness insures instability.

Because of the emotional turmoil instituted by double-mindedness, psychologists are very interested in this phenomenon. Leon Festinger, who researched this concept extensively, calls it "cognitive dissonance."[4] He found that whenever a person holds two contradictory items of information simultaneously, he will be motivated to reduce this discrepancy by modifying his actions or his thinking.

In his classic research study, students were exposed to a boring experiment. Researchers then told them to hype the experiment as very exciting to a new group of participants, and paid them differing amounts of money to do so. The experimenters found that the degree of guilt the subjects experienced was inversely related to the amount of money they received. Subjects who received a lot of money had little trouble exaggerating to the new participants because their payment encouraged rationalization of their behavior. However, those who received small sums of money experienced great dissonance since they were asked to falsify their perceptions for no good reason, and they felt guilty for this behavior. This suggests why otherwise upstanding citizens may be sucked into white collar larceny. They experience little dissonance or guilt since the payoff for these crimes is high and there is no visible suffering victim. These same persons would cringe at the thought of armed robbery or other violent crime.

Jesus warned the Pharisees that divided loyalties between their calling to God and their penchant for materialistic gain were incompatible and would demand a choice. He declared, "No servant can serve two masters. Either he will hate the one and love the other, or he will be devoted to the one and despise the other. You cannot serve both God and Money" (Luke 16:13). This problem remains prominent in Christendom today as the desire for riches often conflicts with dependence on the Lord and service to Him. When money is scarce, thoughts of self-dependence create much dissonance and are quickly dismissed. But when material resources are abundant, double-mindedness is more prevalent. The history of the church is filled with those who reduce the dissonance by subtly aligning their affections with money.

The cure for double-mindedness is a strong allegiance to God and His principles regardless of the circumstances which may tempt us otherwise. This decision is easier to accomplish before a dilemma presents itself. A model is given to us by Joshua, a man renowned for his strong convictions and single-minded devotion to the Lord, even when this demanded giving a minority opinion opposed by his ten fellow spies. Late in his life, after the Children of Israel reclaimed their Promised Land through victories fought under the mighty hand of Jehovah, Joshua assembled the Israelites and asked them to take a single-minded focus. He knew that the pagan gods of the conquered Amorites would tempt his countrymen to dilute their allegiance to Jehovah. So he asked them for a strong commitment while God's battlefield provision for them was still quite fresh. He rehearsed God's goodness to the people, from the call of Abraham to their present victories, and commanded, "Choose for yourselves this day whom you will serve, whether the gods your forefathers served beyond the River, or the gods of the Amorites. . . . But as for me and my household, we will serve the Lord" (Joshua 24:15). We should follow Joshua's example to fight double-mindedness and make our choice for God's principles before the alternatives become attractive. This requires an understanding of His provisions for us and rehearsal of His goodness. A firm, single-minded focus dissuades unrighteous options and the dissonance which accompanies them.

Changing Our Thinking

Since thinking is foundational to our actions and feelings, it follows that detecting and modifying unhelpful thinking patterns is fundamental to psychological health. Too many Christians try to take a shortcut to emotional health by merely putting on a happy face without changing their underlying self-statements. As Job reminds us, this strategy is destined for failure: "If I say, 'I will forget my complaint, I will change my expression, and smile,' I still dread all my sufferings" (Job 9:27-28). Likewise, behavior change without also changing our thoughts is an invitation for the actions to return. This is a basic problem with legalistic submission to rules. For as Colossians 2:23 warns us, self-imposed obedience to regulations without an attitude change is of little value.

The Apostle Paul is the Scripture's most ardent advocate of thinking-alteration. When discussing the proper use of spiritual gifts, he charged the Corinthians, "Stop thinking like children . . . in your thinking be adults" (1 Corinthians

14:20). Later, in describing to this same congregation the divine weapons with which they wage war against unrighteousness, Paul asserted, "We take captive every thought to make it obedient to Christ" (2 Corinthians 10:5). He commanded the Roman Christians to adopt God's perspective by renewing their minds (Romans 12:2), and similarly persuaded the Colossians to change their behaviors by first setting their "minds on things above, not on earthly things" (Colossians 3:2). Paul concluded his most encouraging letter with the exhortation, "Finally, brothers, whatever is true, whatever is noble, whatever is right, whatever is pure, whatever is lovely, whatever is admirable—if anything is excellent or praiseworthy—think about such things" (Philippians 4:8).

Modifying unhealthy thinking is a major task of psychologists, and entire theories of psychotherapeutic change are built around this key ingredient. The process is known as Cognitive Restructuring, since thoughts or cognitions are restructured to produce optimal emotional health. We must first identify our unhelpful thinking and then modify it to reflect more realistic and biblical ideas. It is not necessarily a process of inducing positive thinking. Rather, the goal is to practice the "sober judgment" Paul described in Romans 12:3 so that we might see our situations from the Lord's perspective.

• Identifying unhealthy thinking. Most of us have little difficulty detecting troublesome thoughts like, "I hope my handling of the Smith account doesn't tarnish my chances for promotion," or, "I wonder if I'm being the best parent I can be." However, identifying those irrational thoughts which are deeply ingrained in our usual thinking is much more difficult. We may be oblivious to the errors in our thinking even when they are apparent to those around us. Sometimes our basic assumptions are off-base, infecting our subsequent reasoning and the feelings and actions that emanate from them. Chicken Little really believed the sky was falling, and his behavior and emotions reflected his sincerity. But he was sincerely wrong.

For example, many people have an "ugly duckling complex." Early in life they are fed a constant diet of criticism by parents, teachers, and peers about the way they do things. They believe these negative pronouncements and feel awkward and ugly. They compare themselves unfavorably with others, emphasizing their faults and minimizing their assets. Over time this discouraging self-perspective weaves its way into the fabric of their everyday thinking and colors all their personal evaluations. A benign error such as dialing a wrong phone number or spilling a glass of water is followed by self-demeaning criticisms such as, "I'm so stupid. I can't get anything right!" or, "What a klutz! It's a wonder I can walk and chew bubble gum at the same time." While others may recognize these as overreactions, these individuals are convinced that their pronouncements are accurate. Because their well-ingrained beliefs hold the position of truth, deflated self-esteem, unwillingness to take risks, and negative emotions are certain to follow. It never occurs to them that the water may hold a reflection of a beautiful swan; their strengths are never considered. Detection of this negative thinking is the first step on the journey to health.

Common dysfunctional thoughts are those which contain arbitrary "shoulds" and "should nots." Check your thinking for internal statements such as, "Everyone *should* like me," "I *should* do everything well," or "Things *should not* go wrong in my life." Other problematic thoughts are that we must be in the presence of others to have fun, that people are fragile and must never be made uncomfortable, and that our past experiences unalterably determine our future behaviors and feelings. We should check our conversations with ourselves to see if such thinking has crept in.

Negative thinking may also be detected by investigating categories of irrational beliefs.[5] The following five types of irrational thinking generate a good deal of emotional pain:

1. Blowup thinking—exaggerating or magnifying the meaning of an event out of proportion or generating a rule from a single incident. For example, "I had a strange

thought yesterday—I'm going insane." In such cases, one takes a very small bit of information and assigns enormous importance to it. This often results in unjustifiable leaps in logic and conclusions drawn from very scanty evidence.

2. All-or-nothing thinking—thinking in extremes. All-or-nothing thinkers see only two possibilities: right or wrong, good or bad, black or white, always or never. They have much difficulty seeing any compromise or gray areas in their reasoning. For instance, an all-or-nothing thinker may state, "No one ever has any fun with me," or "I always do poorly in math." This reasoning obscures the alternatives that may be possible and leads to feelings of helplessness.

3. Projective thinking—placing responsibility on others. These persons have difficulty assuming responsibility for their own emotional state or their own personal worth. For example, one may say, "If my mother had spent more time with me, then I would be a more stable person." Shifting responsibility to another person has several negative effects. When we blame others, we tend to make them defensive and to alienate them. When we dwell on the way others have mistreated us, we lessen our ability to find a way out of our negative thinking.

4. Perfectionistic thinking—believing that nothing short of a perfect performance is worthwhile. These persons place on themselves idealistic demands which are very difficult to live up to. For instance, a perfectionistic thinker may say, "Everyone must like me," or "I must always be successful." Because perfection is not attainable, perfectionistic thinkers are constantly dissatisfied.

5. Self-punishing thinking—berating oneself for not performing adequately. Sometimes people become so disappointed with their performance that they lose sight of the task at hand and focus on self-criticism. This results in a poor self-image and in a feeling of hopelessness as defeat seems inevitable. Statements such as, "There's no use in my trying to play golf since I'm never good at athletics," or "I'm so dumb that I'll never learn this material," are self-

punishing thinking. People with this attitude constantly focus on their inadequacies, encouraging further failure.

Take some time to consider your own thinking, especially that which accompanies unpleasant emotions. Do you recognize any of these specific irrational beliefs or any thoughts which fall into these dysfunctional categories? These villains hold our emotions hostage until rescue can be effected by the heroes in the white hats—*cognitive restructuring strategies*.

● Changing unhealthy thinking. The most straightforward attack on irrational thinking is direct confrontation of the belief itself. This frontal assault involves rationally disputing the claims of the negative thinking and presenting evidence for a more realistic perception. Because most troubling thoughts are resistant to surrender, the battle plan must include concerted efforts to claim the beach, enter the main battle with full armament, and root out the retreating beligerents one by one from their hiding places.

Let's take the example of George, a middle-class family man who invested in a company which then failed. George feels depressed and angry at himself. He feels embarrassed when he faces his wife and he senses a distance from God. An investigation of George's thinking reveals the following internal monologue: "Why did I buy that stock? I should have known that company would go belly-up. I can't do anything right! My wife will never trust my financial decisions again, and God is angry with me because I'm such a poor steward of the resources He's given me."

With self-statements like these, it's no wonder George has a gloomy disposition. A rational attack on George's thinking requires evidence that validates or invalidates each of his beliefs. He might ask himself, "Why should I have known the company would fail?" If the answer is that there were obvious danger signs which he ignored, then this thought is rational, and he should criticize his performance. However, if no evidence of decline existed or it was unavailable to him, his belief is harsh and unrealistic.

The rest of George's self-statements are clearly irrational. He asserts that he can't do anything well. This is a gross exaggeration, as can be attested by anyone who knows him and has observed his relationships with his children, his workmanship, or his devotion to God. He laments that his wife will never trust him with the checkbook again, but she originally encouraged him to make the investment when he laid out the idea to her. She's disappointed too, but not with George. He assumes God's anger and pictures Him as the stringent taskmaster interested only in the financial acuity of His children. But this is not the God of the Bible. God loves George for who he is and is far more interested in his growth than in his finances. Even if George has made a careless error, God is faithful and just in forgiving confessed sin.

George must dispute his irrational beliefs repeatedly until they lose their power. He might accomplish this by writing each negative self-statement on a card and listing the more realistic beliefs underneath. Then every time he finds himself engaging in this thinking, he immediately inserts the more rational replacement into the air waves of his mind. Note that the result will not necessarily be elation. George may have ignored warnings to avoid the investment, and his resulting feeling may be frustration with himself. But the exaggerated self-depreciatory thoughts will not be allowed broadcast time because they are untrue. The stronger negative emotions are thus eliminated.

Another way to modify our thinking is through the process of reframing—changing the perspective with which we view our situation. An airline passenger may feel very irritated when she misses her connection until she learns that the plane had to make an emergency landing because of equipment malfunction. Our tastes in clothing are reframed constantly as the neckties that were once too wide or narrow are now so stylish, or the colors that seemed so loud a few years ago now adorn us handsomely. Recognition of God's sovereignty should help Christians reframe their circumstances, but this is not usually our style. We are often like Peter trying to prevent Christ from going to the Cross; we fail to understand the enormous folly of imposing our will on God's plans.

Reframing lifts our spirits as it helps us gain a wider vision of our position and a better understanding of our limitless God. We can frame the seating of a stranger beside us at the church banquet as a misfortune for which we'll pay dearly in discomfort, or as an opportunity to expand our social network and meet an exciting sibling in Christ. Paul reframed his thorn in the flesh as a blessing which kept him dependent on the Lord's power. George, whose financial reversal was described earlier, might reframe the timing of his loss as a blessing since it thwarted his plans to make a substantial purchase of the same stock with his upcoming tax refund.

A final method of cognitive restructuring is through attention diversion. Sometimes concentration on a negative set of circumstances has no redeeming value. This is particularly true when we have no control over the elements that beset us. While in the Philippian jail, Paul and Silas could sing hymns at midnight because they dwelt upon God's goodness instead of on their miserable predicament.

Attention diversion was the advice of Maria, the delightful governess of the Von Trapp children in *The Sound of Music*, when she saw the fearfulness of her young charges during a thunderstorm. She rightly noticed that their focus was on the loud thunderclaps, the bright streaks of lightning in the sky, and the heavy downpour of rain. These elements seemed quite foreboding to the children. However, Maria recognized the importance of a mental focus in determining feelings, and she encouraged the children to turn their attention to their favorite things. After cataloging many positive thoughts from her experiences, such as brown paper packages tied up with strings, or snowflakes that accumulate on her nose and eyelashes, she sings to the children that these thoughts easily divert her attention from dog bites, bee stings, and other negative experiences.

SEVEN

*"Be very careful, then, how you live—not
as unwise but as wise, making the most
of every opportunity."*
Ephesians 5:15-16

Plan Your Life

A strong adolescent hired himself out to split wood in order to earn some spending money. He worked diligently the first day and was quite productive. The same was true the second day and so he accepted several wood-chopping assignments. As the week progressed, the young man's production began to decline. He decided to work even harder, but his extra effort would not reverse the slide. As he worked frantically to fulfill his commitments, an older woodcutter observed the young man's plight and asked him, "When did you last sharpen your ax?" It seems the boy had been working so hard that he had forgotten to maintain his equipment.

How often do we work harder instead of smarter? The computer greets us with the same error message each time we refuse to consult the manual and instead reenter the ill-fated commands. We roam around the countryside wasting hours because we failed to map out precise directions to our destination before leaving home. Or we visit the supermarket daily because we don't take the time to inspect our cupboards and generate a grocery list once a week.

Organizing our lives and managing our time are essential skills for insuring emotional health. When we fail to structure our lives, we feel overwhelmed by obligations. When we manage our time and other resources, we feel a sense of control over our lives. This translates into positive self-esteem, alleviation of stress, and freedom to devote energy to righteous behavior.

Goal-Setting

If we aim at nothing, we'll be sure to hit it. However, when we set personal goals, we sharpen our focus and give direction to our behavior. When we refuse to clarify our goals, we invite others to decide what's important for us.

Spiritual goals are necessary for appropriate service to God. Jesus perfectly illustrated this point as He conducted His Father's business. He always focused on His appointed work, even when His approaching execution stirred such agony that He perspired blood. The Apostle Paul was clear about his goal. He wrote to the Philippians:

> *Not that I have already obtained all this, or have already been made perfect, but I press on to take hold of that for which Christ Jesus took hold of me. Brothers, I do not consider myself yet to have taken hold of it. But one thing I do: Forgetting what is behind and straining toward what is ahead, I press on toward the goal to win the prize for which God has called me heavenward in Christ Jesus. (3:12-14)*

When our goals are firmly set in allegiance to Jehovah, we find it easier to refuse the king's meat, as Daniel did, and also to worship God openly. Like Gideon, we can trust God for victories when the odds against us seem overwhelming. When those around us can only ridicule, we can act in obedience, as Noah did when he built an ark in a world without rain. Firm spiritual goals produce consistency of character.

Goals are no less important in the other dimensions of our lives. Women willingly subject their bodies to pregnancy and delivery because the goal of childbearing supercedes any discomfort.

Goals affect our attitudes and feelings as well. The world-class runner who finishes the Boston Marathon in eighth place and the sixty-two-year-old businessman who completes the course in the bottom fourth of racers will likely have different emotional reactions inversely related to their timed performances. The athlete may feel frustrated because his goal was a first-place finish, while the businessman may be ecstatic because his goal was merely to make it to the finish line.

We should identify both short- and long-term goals to direct our actions. It is most helpful if we place these targets in writing. These include spiritual commitments, family objectives, vocational ambitions, financial strivings, and social pursuits. We should review our goals regularly to guard against the tyranny of the urgent which could sidetrack us. Along with each goal, it is beneficial to list the activities which contribute to goal attainment and identify as many avenues for fulfillment as possible. Goals should be realistic and open to modification when new information or spiritual guidance indicates the need for change.

Prioritizing

Nothing is so inefficient as the careful completion of a task that doesn't need to be done. And yet we've all fallen into the trap of spending energy on projects that have little value. Managers neatly arrange and rearrange the paper clips and pencils in their desk drawers; students type their "to do" lists but don't "do." When we fail to prioritize goals, our efforts are often as futile as rearranging the deck chairs on the *Titanic*.

The importance of setting priorities is illustrated by the strategies employed by novice and expert chess players. A new competitor inevitably focuses on capturing as many of his opponent's pieces as possible. The seasoned chess veteran keys on an opponent's king and captures pieces only when they bear directly on self-protection or compromise the safety of the enemy monarch.

We need to consider the relative importance of the goals

and tasks we face. This demands thoughtful prioritizing. Goals should be categorized in primary, secondary, or tertiary levels of importance to guide our resource allocation to each one. This helps us resist the urge to tackle less important tasks initially, even though they may be easier to complete and check off our "to do" lists. This also insures God of His proper place in the hierarchy of our thinking. Just as Jesus taught His followers about their concern over food and clothing, we should "seek first [the Father's] kingdom and His righteousness, and all these things will be given to [us] as well" (Matthew 6:33).

Planning

A well-known business axiom states, "To fail to plan is to plan to fail." Careful planning is helpful for a number of reasons. It provides guidelines for completing tasks and reduces inactivity and misdirected energy expenditure. It diminishes our feeling of being overwhelmed by a chore. A plan allows us to take one thing at a time instead of scattering our efforts. Planning enhances our effectiveness. The major difference between the papers turned in by college and high school students is not attributable to any vastly superior intelligence of the college student, but rather to the time committed to construction of an outline. High school students tend to develop their outlines after the paper is written, simply because the teacher demands to see one, while college students typically formulate the outline first to guide their writing.

The Christian life demands thoughtful planning. Jesus warned His listeners that those who called Him "Lord" must put His words into action. Using the analogy of builders in Luke 6:48-49, Jesus contrasted persons who structure their lives around His teaching with those who hear His words but fail to plan their lives in accordance. He said that the wise builder is "like a man building a house who dug down deep and laid the foundation on rock. When a flood came, the torrent struck that house but could not shake it, because it was well built." The unstructured individual is "like a man who built a house on the ground without a foundation. The moment the torrent struck that house, it collapsed and its destruction was complete."

Likewise, Jesus warned against a laissez-faire attitude in regard to following Him, and He clearly identified the importance of planning:

> *Suppose one of you wants to build a tower. Will he not first sit down and estimate the cost to see if he has enough money to complete it? For if he lays the foundation and is not able to finish it, everyone who sees it will ridicule him, saying, "This fellow began to build and was not able to finish."*
>
> *Or suppose a king is about to go to war against another king. Will he not first sit down and consider whether he is able with ten thousand men to oppose the one coming against him with twenty thousand? If he is not able, he will send a delegation while the other is still a long way off and will ask for terms of peace. In the same way, any of you who does not give up everything he has cannot be My disciple. (Luke 14:28-33)*

The first consideration in any planning activity should be its adherence to biblical principles. Solomon said, "Commit to the Lord whatever you do, and your plans will succeed. . . . When a man's ways are pleasing to the Lord, He makes even his enemies live at peace with him" (Proverbs 16:3, 7). Conversely, failure to consider the Lord's perspective can doom even the most ingenious schemes. "There is no wisdom, no insight, no plan that can succeed against the Lord" (Proverbs 21:30).

Most effective planners commit their plans to writing and include their objectives and time estimates for completing the required work. Large tasks should be broken down into manageable components with clear instructions for each step. Small manageable tasks which have visible end points are more readily attempted than larger ones even when the megatask is an obvious compilation of many microtasks. After all, a marathon is run one step at a time.

Even the most extraordinary plans are of no use if they are not followed. For this reason, it is imperative to review our plans regularly for guidance. Most management consultants recommend that we devote at least ten minutes at the beginning and end of each day to plan our daily tasks and assess our progress. Plans should be flexible in case problems develop and changes are warranted. Even the most beautifully designed and crafted bumper stickers will not sell if the candidate whose name appears on them fails to receive his party's nomination for the office.

Managing Our Time

Perhaps our most valuable personal resource is time. The quality of our lives reflects of our decisions concerning the use of this fleeting commodity. Paul admonishes us to make "the most of every opportunity" (Ephesians 5:16), and James compares our lives to a mist which quickly vanishes (James 4:14). Time utilization is not an issue which we can ignore, for failure to exercise control over this resource results in either its waste or deference to the wishes of others.

A frequent objection to time management is that these actions reduce life's spontaneity and curtail freedom. The truth of the matter appears to be quite the opposite. People who do not plan are not as much free as they are reactionary. Life demands that attention be given to physical, social, and emotional needs. Instead of organizing for the fulfillment of these needs, the unstructured individual simply *reacts* to the motivation that screams the loudest, or approaches deadlines frantically in an effort to reach a goal.

Some complain that they have too much to do already, and time management is merely another activity vying for space on an overcrowded docket. This is akin to saying that a car's premature engine overhaul is more cost effective than regular oil changes. In reality, efforts spent in time management pay for themselves many times over in the freedom they provide to engage in desired activities.

● Scheduling. A successful baseball manager begins each season by getting to know the strengths and weaknesses of his players before instituting changes. An effective time manager does the same. Assess your current time usage by monitoring several twenty-four-hour intervals and recording your activities for each hour. Identify your productive uses of time as well as the unnecessary activities in which you engage.

Next fill out a proposed personal schedule which realistically takes into account the tasks you need to complete and the time parameters necessary to achieve them. Most people underestimate the time required to complete a task, so observe the "plus ten" rule. Add at least ten minutes to the projected schedule for every nonroutine activity. If you happen to finish on time, use the ten minutes to prepare for the next task or simply to relax.

Now look over your schedule and rate each task as to the amount of energy and activity it demands. Work should be spaced neatly throughout the day. It is not good to stack all the simple activities in the morning and the more grueling ones in the afternoon. Also be sure to list alternate tasks that may be substituted for planned tasks which become impossible to attempt.

Another useful scheduling tip is to observe the 10 o'clock principle: "Eat a bullfrog for breakfast and nothing worse will happen to you for the remainder of the day." This simply means that if you achieve your most distasteful task by 10 A.M. each day, the rest of the day will be more satisfying. When you put off your dreaded chores, you create added anxiety because not only do you have to complete the dastardly deed, but you also must deal with the negative anticipation of this action. So do that paperwork, make that call, or mow the grass early in the day and avoid the double dose of stress.

● Setting limits. Remember the last time you had one of

those weeks when something was going on every night. You chaired a meeting one evening, coached softball the next, then choir practice, that late business call, your daughter's recital, and all day Saturday was spent at the seminar. You hardly had time to sleep. We all have weeks like this, and each time we vow never to overcommit again.

We needn't look far for the source of our exhaustion, for we are our own culprits. We often act as if we are exempt from the time constraints of the twenty-four-hour day. Sadly, our closest relationships are usually the victims of this overzealous scheduling as activities invade the time we should be devoting to God and our families. Consider your last hectic week and you'll probably recognize that your devotions suffered. Even when we curb our own passion for overcommitment, other people will gladly find plenty of projects to fill our schedules.

Limit-setting demands that we determine the relative importance of tasks so that we make good choices, not just convenient ones. We must resist personal perceptions of omnipotence and recognize that even worthwhile projects may need to be bypassed when there's not enough time. Jesus had tremendous compassion for the sick, and He loved to teach His countrymen; but on several occasions He dismissed those who were waiting for Him so He might engage in communion with His Father and fellowship with His disciples.

Requiring personal perfection also prevents us from setting realistic limits. The perfectionist has difficulty finishing a project and turning his attention to another. There always seems to be another detail requiring time. Anything approaching perfection is rarely attainable or necessary. A good job is usually sufficient. We need to take control of our expectations and set realistic limits.

• Avoid fighting the clock. Many times we make a task harder by depriving ourselves of the time needed to complete it. The student crams all night for the next day's test. The churchgoer drives frantically to the service after leaving home too late and feels anything but worshipful. The office worker keeps one eye on the clock, sweating the deadline of a report that has been sitting on the desk all week. The clock is a relentless adversary and it usually wins when we put things off.

Procrastination is a common time-management concern. Far too often we underestimate the amount of time a task will require and start working on it late instead of early. We fail to allot any time for the inevitable interferences that arise, putting us further behind. Any assignment becomes drudgery when it must be performed in a shrunken time capsule. We are more prone to procrastinate on jobs that are distasteful. Our aversion for the task, coupled with the deadline looming over us, makes its completion almost impossible and precludes any chance of performance up to our potential. This is why some doctoral students finish all their grueling coursework but never get their degree. The last requirement is a dissertation which usually must be completed in a set amount of time. The writing of this technical book seems so foreboding that they procrastinate and fail to finish by their degree deadline. I have never met a doctoral student who planned to meet all requirements except dissertation, but this procrastination causes many doctoral casualties.

I struggled with procrastination when I first began my professional practice of psychology. I very much like to talk with people and help them with their problems, but I very much dislike writing the professional reports about each session. As a young psychologist I ventured out of my office between counseling sessions to stretch my legs or get a drink of water. Inevitably, I became sidetracked from writing my notes; it seemed so much easier to converse with a colleague down the hall or return to make a phone call while I had a few minutes. I told myself that there was plenty of time to record the note before my next client. As you might guess, when I finally began writing, precious little time remained to complete the charts, and interruptions frequently prevented me from doing them before the next session. This meant that I stayed later in the evening trying to reconstruct the counseling sessions in order to complete the records. This made the chore significantly more difficult.

I solved the procrastination problem by timing how long it took me to complete my notes on each client. After getting this realistic time assessment, I determined to make the entries immediately after the client left my office, closing the door behind him to keep me in and interferences out. After writing the notes I was free to engage in any activity I desired without the guilt of knowing I was shirking a responsibility. My records became more complete, my attitude improved, and I left for home much earlier.

Tips for Effective Resource Management
There's a lot of truth to the old adage, "Time is money." For this reason seminars and workshops on time management abound in the business community. The ideas are transferable to nonwork settings as well, helping us maximize our efficiency in every aspect of our lives. Detailed below are some of the tips I find effective for optimal time management:

• Analyze your use of time and determine which activities are your time wasters. On what do you spend considerable time without comparable benefits? You should try to identify and eliminate one time waster a week.

• Prioritize your goals, put them in writing, and position the list in a conspicuous place. You have a much better chance of meeting goals when they are fresh on your mind.

• Tackle the hardest assignments first. Observe the 10 o'clock principle described earlier and take the dread out of your day.

• Define your tasks before you begin working on them. It's amazing how often we stagnate, trying to determine how we should proceed or go diligently in the wrong direction simply because we are unclear about the assignment.

• Periodically schedule empty blocks of time to deal with unexpected occurrences or to catch up when you get behind. If you are right on schedule, take a break—you've earned it!

• Delegate tasks to others when you can. You don't have to do everything yourself. Others can learn to do a job only when they are given the opportunity to try it on their own. Many children of skilled craftsmen can't even drive a nail straight because their parents never let them help.

• Always give credit and praise to yourself and others for a job well done or for extra effort. Family members, friends, and coworkers will enjoy helping you when you are encouraging.

• Try to handle each piece of paper that comes across your desk just once. For instance, when you look through your mail, discard any item for which you have no specific file or place. If it demands an answer, reply while the issues are fresh on your mind. If it contains useful information, underscore the important points so you will not have to reread the entire text the next time you refer to it.

• Do only one thing at a time. When you begin multiple projects, you usually wind up with multiple incompletions. Working on one assignment allows you to focus intently on what needs to be done and prevents you from being sidetracked.

• Give priority to devotional time with God. Don't fall into the trap of thinking you're too busy working *for* God to spend time *with* Him. Gaining spiritual refreshment enhances all of our other pursuits and helps us recognize when they deviate from God's principles.

SECTION 3

The two emotions which most often bring people into my counseling office are anger and depression. Everyone has bouts with these feelings, but sometimes they seem so overwhelming that other issues fade in comparison. They demand immediate attention and refuse to go away if ignored.

Anger is a misunderstood emotion that is present in all of our lives. It generates an intense physical reaction and makes us uncomfortable until we do something about it. The problem is that unbridled expression of this emotion often carries significant social consequences.

Depression, though, is a more insidious problem. There are many more degrees of this emotion and its origins do not seem nearly as clear-cut as those of anger. Depression affects our whole being and deflates our outlook and motivation. When we're depressed, we just want to feel better, but often are powerless to pull ourselves up again. Prolonged depression diminishes our hope.

I believe that these two emotions are intricately associated. Anger turned inward becomes depression. When we become angry with ourselves and fail to negotiate a resolution, we can only maintain the tense state for so long before it is relegated to depression. We may also become angry at ourselves for failing to express our negative feelings to others and, again, take it out on ourselves through a deflated mood. Unfortunately, unresolved anger does not merely dissipate as some seem to believe. Of course, depression can arise from many other sources, but personal anger is often an overlooked origin.

Chapter 8 deals with anger—its universal presence and its position in God's scheme for us. Chapter 9 examines depression—its symptoms and prevalence. Practical strategies for managing each of these emotions are then provided.

EIGHT

"In your anger do not sin."
Psalm 4:4

Face Your Anger

How do you feel when a motorist carelessly cuts closely in front of you, forcing you to apply your brakes? When your preschooler spills her milk all over the floor, after repeated warnings to move her cup? When a confessed murderer escapes penalty because of a legal technicality? Or when you blow a very makable putt for par.

If we're honest with ourselves, we'll have to admit that at least some of these situations tend to trigger tightness in our stomachs, a quickened pulse, and warmth around the collar. The emotion is anger and the physical changes are triggered automatically. It is a strong feeling of displeasure in reaction to some aversive event or idea. Anger may be directed toward those who misbehave, toward ourselves for perceived inadequacies, or even toward God. It is an emotion that arrests our attention quickly and resists leaving quietly.

Although anger is an emotion, it usually keeps close company with a whole array of unkind behaviors. Angry children throw temper tantrums. Angry adolescents answer sarcastically. Angry adults speak in stern tones and evidence tense muscles. When we're angry, we feel like throwing objects, hitting someone, or giving others a choice piece of our minds. And more times than we'd like to admit, we act aggressively when we're mad.

Anger is a common emotion. It has been identified as one of the first discernable feelings experienced by infants. The Scriptures record a very early presence of this emotion in human history, when Cain, the first person ever born into the world, became so angry with his brother that he murdered him. Unrighteous actions have accompanied anger throughout human history. In fact, many see this emotion as a legitimate excuse for all types of misbehavior. People say, "I was just so mad that I couldn't control myself."

Anger arises in response to perceived injustices and disappointed expectations. We become angry when we attribute dishonest motives to others or catch someone lying. We get our dander up when others are inconsiderate, careless, or brutal. Observing sinful behavior can generate a good deal of ire, as when standards of decency are eroding in our communities. Anger at ourselves and those closest to us is generally provoked by our disappointed expectations. We're mad at ourselves for getting lost in a part of town we should know. A spouse arouses anger when she fails to follow through on a task she had agreed to do. Disappointed expectations are usually the reason people become angry at God. They feel let down because He didn't shield them from catastrophe or meet their needs as they desired. In essence, anger always eminates from a discrepancy between how things are and how we think they ought to be.

Angry People in the Bible

In the Scriptures, accounts of angry people abound. Moses was no stranger to this emotion. The thankless task of leading the entire Jewish nation on their journey through the wilderness fell to this patriarch. The people complained perpetually about inconveniences and dissatisfaction with his leadership, exacting a tremendous toll of energy from Moses.

God's personal delivery of the Law to Moses is a major

theme of the Book of Exodus. However, even while this transaction was taking place, the Israelites constructed a golden calf for worship in Moses' absence. Exodus 32 describes the events surrounding Moses' discovery of this idolatry. He was so enraged with this unrighteousness that he dashed the tablets engraved by God onto the ground.

Later at Kadesh the Children of Israel gathered in opposition to Moses and Aaron because they lacked sufficient water to meet their needs. The people griped about their thirst and lamented that they were not left in Egyptian slavery where water and a variety of foods were plentiful. The Lord told Moses to speak to the rock and He would provide abundant water for the congregation. Moses could hardly be faulted for being weary of his ungrateful charges. But he became so indignant that he called them rebels and struck the rock twice with his staff, claiming that he would provide their precious water. For this disobedience, Moses was not allowed to accompany them into the Promised Land.

The anger of many other biblical characters is also recorded. However, it is God who most often expresses anger. For instance, He too became fed up with Moses' disgruntled followers: "Now the people complained about their hardships in the hearing of the Lord, and when He heard them His anger was aroused. Then fire from the Lord burned among them" (Numbers 11:1).

The Apostle John tells of Jesus' consuming wrath when He found the temple area transformed from a place of worship into a market. In His zeal He overturned the tables of the money changers and drove the merchants out. Jesus' anger was most often directed at the smug religious leaders who' misrepresented His Father. Jesus called woes down on the Pharisees and teachers of the Law and referred to them as snakes and whitewashed tombs. He became particularly annoyed when these self-serving ministers tried to entrap Him in actions which violated their traditions. Mark records one such incidence in which these leaders located a disabled man at the synagogue and scrutinized Jesus to see if He would heal on the Sabbath. Mark reports that Jesus healed the man but was angry and deeply distressed at their stubborn hearts which refused to acknowledge Him as the Christ.

It's interesting that even though anger is ascribed to God twice as often as it is to humans, the emotion is viewed negatively almost every time people in the Bible experienced it. Apparently, the emotion itself is not a sin, but we have a great deal of difficulty managing this emotion righteously. Our track record is so bad that anger is frequently listed among emotions to be avoided (for example, Psalm 37:8; Colossians 3:8). Most of us know persons who desperately need to heed this advice!

Solomon took a particular interest in anger. He suggested that one's rate of response one has to an annoying situation is a key to discerning how wise a person is. Speed is inversely related to wisdom. That means that a person who responds quickly in anger is said to be foolish while one who shows more patience is wise. Which verse applies to you? Proverbs 12:16, "A fool shows his annoyance at once"? Or Proverbs 19:11, "A man's wisdom gives him patience; it is to his glory to overlook an offense"?

I find that quick-tempered people have difficulty recognizing their foolishness. Their impassioned rhetoric serves only to instill their convictions more deeply. This further insulates them from competing explanations of events and their foolishness is perpetuated. Hot-tempered people are full of excuses for their short fuses. Unfortunately, a bad day at work, monthly hormonal imbalances, or following in your father's footsteps may sound good to you, but they don't play well to your listeners.

Conversely, less hasty responses demonstrate wisdom. The more cautious we are in exploring a situation that may even initially evoke anger, the more objective we can be. Resisting an immediate angry expression also gives us more time to consider our options and modify our behavior. Solomon applauds overlooking an insult and turning anger away.

• The final outcome. Anger left undetected and untreated can be a devastating force. Proverbs 27:4 characterizes anger as "cruel" and its resultant fury as "overwhelming." Anger can permeate every facet of our personality if left unchecked. I have worked with patients who were so angry at an individual they could not control their emotions or actions. Their constant processing of perceived injustices and plots of retribution distracted them from other pursuits, and soon the hated person was exerting a tremendous influence over them by monopolizing their time and energy. Solomon described this pitiful person, "Like a city whose walls are broken down is a man who lacks self-control" (Proverbs 25:28). Remember that an unwalled city is more dangerous to those living inside than outside.

Since anger is cruel, strife often accompanies encounters with angry people. Proverbs 29:22 warns, "An angry man stirs up dissension, and a hot-tempered one commits many sins." Most of us have experienced this negative influence of an angry person. When we're around angry people, we feel more irritated ourselves. We tend to become more impassioned about the issue at hand or feel annoyed by the temper we see displayed.

Solomon recognized how difficult it is to quell a quick temper. He said, "A hot-tempered man must pay the penalty; if you rescue him, you will have to do it again" (Proverbs 19:19). The consequences of an uncontrollable temper can be severe. Prisons are filled with persons who have trouble simmering down when upset. I have worked with many men who were losing their wives through actual or emotional divorce and who were pushing their children further away each day because they wouldn't adjust the hair trigger on their anger. I am often amazed at how frequently they promise impulse control and so soon afterward throw another distancing tantrum.

• Solomon's advice. Israel's wisest monarch focused his advice on averting anger in our interpersonal relationships. Because this emotion spreads so rampantly, the best place to quench its fire is at its onset. Solomon likened starting a quarrel to breaching a dam, and advised that we "drop the matter before a dispute breaks out" (Proverbs 17:14).

Perhaps we are calm and complacent, but those around us are full of ire. It is best to quiet the storm through tactful communication. Words are very powerful. Gentle responses make it more difficult for a foe to maintain a heated posture, but harsh words have exactly the opposite effect. Most parents have watched in dismay as their children generate hostile criticisms of each other and masterfully escalate their quarrels. Unfortunately, we are not so attuned to the same progression of hostility arising from ill-chosen words we employ in our own conversations. A word for the wise is a carefully chosen word indeed.

There are some folks who seem always to be mad, and our most polished responses do little to appease them. If you've met a person like this, you'll never forget him—even though you'll probably try. Solomon offers specific advice for managing this predicament: "Do not make friends with a hot-tempered man, do not associate with one easily angered, or you may learn his ways and get yourself ensnared" (Proverbs 22:24-25).

The Biblical Verdict

Since anger is a universal emotion, experienced by God as well as humans, it is difficult to condemn outright, because God's behavior is above reproach. I believe that anger can best be understood by examining God's anger. We have the capacity for this emotion because of our creation in His image.

God's anger is always in response to unrighteousness. He hates sin and becomes indignant when transgressions of His Law abound. Isaiah described this characteristic of God:

> *Woe to those who call evil good and good evil,*
> *who put darkness for light and light for darkness,*
> *who put bitter for sweet and sweet for bitter.*
> *Woe to those who are wise in their own eyes*

and clever in their own sight.
Woe to those who are heroes at drinking wine
and champions at mixing drinks, who acquit the
guilty for a bribe, but deny justice to the inno-
cent. . . .
For they have rejected the law of the Lord Almighty
and spurned the word of the Holy One of Israel.
Therefore the Lord's anger burns against His people.
(Isaiah 5:20-25)

Similarly, we become angry in response to a violation of our standards or expectations. No one is angry when he gets his own way. A parent can prevent a child's temper tantrums merely by giving in to his every whim. The child fumes because he labels his mother's refusal to let him play in the street as an affront to his own happiness. The angry husband derides his wife because her choices for allocating the resources in their joint checking account do not coincide with his.

Anger is triggered in all of us when we perceive an injustice. Herein lies the problem—our personal definitions of unrighteousness do not jibe with God's. Many times they are not even close. We may view a heinous murder just as God does and respond with indignation over the crime. But when we take a few minutes to consider our typical bouts with anger, we may notice a much-less-than divine standard being applied. Joe's forgetting to call was hardly immoral. Sally's preference for a different restaurant doesn't qualify for divine retribution. Little Jimmy's sloppy eating habits may not be heavenly, but they aren't from hell either. The fact is that most of our anger arises because our selfish standards are violated. The triggering mechanism is not another's sin against *God*, but rather sin against *us.*

The Problem of Control

Even when we become angry because of the violation of a scriptural principle, we're still held accountable for our consequent actions. Perhaps the most often quoted biblical teaching on anger is given in both Psalm 4:4 and Ephesians 4:26: "In your anger do not sin." This is a hard saying because we are less capable of controlling our actions when we're mad than at just about any other time. Sinful actions resulting from anger include hasty judgments of motives, verbal jabs, physical abuse, seeking vengeance, dwelling on the offense, and refusing to offer forgiveness. Indeed anger is one letter short of danger.

Many Christians recognize the pitfalls inherent in flirting with anger and resolve to avoid it altogether. However, this is impossible. Anger is a built-in human emotion and is not eliminated through an "angerectomy." Merely denying or ignoring this feeling doesn't make it disappear. In fact, this strategy may have serious health consequences. Most of us know how eating our anger works on our stomachs; it also does serious damage to our hearts and immune systems. Researchers have identified *anger-in*—the unwillingness to express angry emotions—as a key personality characteristic of coronary patients.[6] Similarly, researchers have found that the tendency to hide one's true feelings—particularly negative ones—is associated with higher cancer rates.[7]

The most appropriate response to anger appears to be one of control rather than denial. This may involve eliminating a constant source of ire, changing our perceptions of events, or modifying our expectations. After anger is triggered, we must learn to express it appropriately. Control also demands that we harness our angry actions and employ them to remove injustices or to strengthen relationships with others. Perhaps the most difficult aspect of dealing with anger is learning to forgive ourselves and others for violating our standards. The balance of this chapter is devoted to these practical topics.

An Ounce of Prevention

Dealing with anger is a lot like handling a forest fire. Like a large forest, we are comprised of many combustible areas which need only a spark of anger to kindle a blaze. And that spark can be generated from many sources. Sometimes careless people ignite our fires by failing to extinguish their campfires of false assumptions, discarding their lighted cigarettes of selfish actions, or playing with their matches of thoughtless errors. Other sparks come from natural and uncontrollable sources. The lightning of disease or death ignites many flames. Some fires are deliberately set by people who purpose to injure us and destroy the forest. We may encourage fires by failing to clear out the dried brush of unrealistic expectations or by blocking the roads through barriers in communication so others are prevented from aiding us in extinguishing the blaze.

Sometimes fires are helpful by consuming decaying forest areas of unmotivation to speak out against immorality and making way for the new vegetation of a righteous witness. But these positive results very rarely occur except under conditions of carefully controlled burning. Fires easily get out of hand and tend to gather momentum as they progress unchecked. They become nondiscriminate in their destruction, consuming the objects closest at hand. It is much more cost- and energy-efficient to prevent a forest fire than to control its raging; that should be our strategy for managing anger as well.

• Early detection. We can control our anger only after it is identified, and the earlier the detection, the better. Every second is critical because of the explosive nature of this emotion and because of our inherent wiring which encourages rapid combustion. This requires vigilance if we are to nip it in the bud.

We must learn to recognize our characteristic ways of responding to anger. Physical symptoms such as elevated heart rate, perspiration, and clenched fists will indicate the diagnosis. The voice level increases in pitch and volume, concentration diminishes, and we tend to think in exaggerated terms. Self-monitoring of these signs should alert us to be on guard.

Early detection of situations liable to raise our dander is equally important. Anger doesn't fall on us from the sky but is precipitated by events. Many anger-provoking incidents are quite predictable, because every time they occur we get mad.

I once counseled a man whose presenting problem was a hot, uncontrollable temper. I asked him what made him mad and he responded, "I just don't know." So I gave him an assignment to keep a record of the events just before he popped his cork. Interestingly, he was able to identify three recurring themes—arguments with his teenage son about the boy's appearance, issues surrounding the family finances, and a certain aspect of his employment. These situations accounted for about ninety percent of his anger. As he discovered his anger producers, he learned to brace himself and head off the feelings.

Sometimes the precipitator of ire is not a specific event but rather a person who regularly irritates us. We should learn to expect negative things from some people. Indeed, our failure to predict annoyance only serves to intensify the negative feelings because our expectations of civility or courteous behavior from them is dashed once again. We must learn from experience. Samson should not have been surprised when Delilah cut his hair, because she carried out every other scheme that he indicated would sap his strength. Prediction provides the earliest detection system.

● Don't think that! Our perceptions and expectations determine whether we become angry or not. If we don't expect our spouse to clean off the table, it won't make us mad when she doesn't. The two means available to us to prevent anger are changing the world to suit us or changing our view of the world. The latter is the easier task.

Christians should ask themselves if the events which make them angry also anger God. If the event is merely a personal inconvenience, our reaction may be the only thing that's unrighteous. This is the anger we are implored so often in the New Testament epistles to put away.

A source of an enormous amount of anger is our tendency to read unpleasant actions by others as personal affronts. Too often we go about looking for an offense. When we take personally Mary's general remark about women working outside of the home, we are much more likely to get mad. Think of your own conversations. We all can remember a remark we made which hurt someone even though we did not intend it to be hurtful. Likewise, others do not consider all possible interpretations of their comments before saying them.

We often get mad at ourselves because we fail to attain personal perfection. Unreasonable demands for success are sure to be disappointed, and our intolerance for mistakes will sentence us to many terms of anger without parole. We think, "I'm so stupid for making that wrong turn," "I'll never learn to keep my head down when I swing at the ball," or "I should never make an error in the checkbook." We're wrong on all counts. Simply agreeing with God that we are fallible will help prevent these bouts of anger.

Whenever we catch ourselves in this unhealthy self-talk, we need to bring on a bucket brigade of realistic thinking to douse the fire that is sure to be kindling. We do not have to think in these negative ways just because we have learned to. That's good news because we can relearn to do otherwise. Proverbs tells us that it is a glory to overlook an offense, and that applies to the offenses we perceive from ourselves and others. Remember the strategies detailed in chapter 6 for changing our thinking.

Self-statements such as, "What am I getting so uptight about? It's no big deal," and "Hey, anyone can get lost in an unfamiliar town," will avert avalanches of anger. Even when the violated standard is righteous and we deserve to get mad, anticipatory self-statements can go a long way to moderate our feelings. Prepare with thoughts like, "It's a shame that he acts that way, but I will not stoop to his level," and "She always does something to get my goat, but I'll be ready for it tonight. I'll just expect some misbehavior and won't be surprised when the inevitable happens." These detection and rethinking skills prevent or keep anger in check early in the cycle.

• Get it out. Expression of anger is as sensitive as handling a case of dynamite in your living room. Placing it too closely to the fire begs for catastrophe. When even one stick is ignited, the whole case blows and the destruction is evident to all. People with short fuses explode quickly and leave a path of interpersonal devastation in their wake. Their anger ignites the anger of others and the harm is multiplied.

Perhaps you don't like having dynamite in your living room and wish to dispose of it quietly. You could wait until the neighbors are out, take it to the cellar, close all the doors, and detonate it secretly. Nobody would hear the explosion. But over time the foundation of your house would tell the story as it cracked and faltered under the intense, enclosed pressure. So it is with people who put on a happy face, sit on their feelings, and let their stomachs take the punishment. While everyone may laud them as great Christians, they pay a high price for this distinction.

A more efficient way to use your dynamite is to store it safely in a noncombustible container. When your work calls for an explosive, carry the sticks carefully to their destination, warn others of your intentions, set adequate fuses, and discharge the dynamite. People who handle anger correctly stay rational even when mad and direct their feelings toward appropriate people or objects without injuring bystanders.

Admittedly, the expression of anger is a risky business. The emotion itself is so intense that it's sometimes difficult to keep a realistic (much less a godly) perspective. Even when expressed admirably, many people are so frightened by any indication of annoyance that they retreat from us immediately. Since there is a social cost for angry expressions, even the most elegantly stated acknowledgment of irritation may not be judicious. We would not tell a boss we're mad at her while asking for a raise or express ire at a spouse while entertaining guests. Like all communication, the expression of anger should be sensitive to the social context.

Anger needs to be expressed to cleanse it from our systems. Repression of this emotion is only a temporary solution since anger we sit on festers and will eventually explode. Sadly, it usually chooses the times we're with our loved ones to expose itself—even when they had nothing to do with its onset. When we fail to handle angry situations when they occur, we lose the opportunity to resolve the issue while the circumstances are clearly out in the open. Situations are difficult to re-create for others at a later time. Also when too much time elapses before the air is cleared, we tend to escalate the significance of offenses.

When you notice anger building inside and determine that the social climate is ripe for its expression, you should keep these guidelines in mind:

1. Take time to formulate what you'll say before you say it. You can cool down by counting to ten, but it may be more effective to use those ten seconds to think through what you're going to say. Ask God for wisdom in shaping your reply. Hasty words can rob you of a night's sleep.

2. If possible, admit your emotion to the one who prompted it. Your close friends or spouse may be willing to listen as you share your irritation at your uncle, but that's all they can do. Your uncle has the power to change his behavior if you communicate with him directly. You will also be more intense when expressing anger directly and more likely to get it all out. If the target of your anger is not accessible, or the cost of a direct response is too high, try journaling exactly how you feel and why.

3. Be honest in your communication. Don't say, "I'm a little annoyed," when you mean, "I'm very angry." I often restate a client's mild angry response more forcefully and ask him to repeat after me. If I am correct that he was minimizing anger, he seems relieved that I won't help him gloss over his feelings.

4. Instead of blaming another for your emotion or concentrating on scoring points against him, take responsibility for your emotion. Replace "you" messages with "I" messages. When you tell Sally, "You really made me mad

by telling that story," you invite a defensive response. She may say, "Don't blame me. It's the truth, you know." Instead, take responsibility for your feeling. You might say, "I feel angry every time I hear that story." Don't give others excessive power over you.

5. Never be afraid to express your feelings to God. Remember, He already knows them anyway. Confess your anger to your Heavenly Father and ask for His comfort and encouragement.

But I Want To Do Something

Anger keys us up for action by initiating the stress response. We experience the adrenaline flow and want to do something, and quick! If unchecked, that something can be very harmful. Who of us hasn't felt the fist clench when a spouse criticizes the handling of the children? That's a natural reaction. It's sin only if we follow through with the swing. However, if our anger stirs us to rescue a victim from the local bully, we applaud the extra strength our bodies appropriate.

Physical exercise will often help dissipate anger, for it burns off the chemicals that are fueling the muscular fire. Beating a punching bag and running briskly are especially appropriate for defusing anger. I often prescribe these exercises to my clients and ask them to visualize their feelings about the offense with every delivery of the glove or pounding of the foot. This expression of anger can calm us down enough to think more rationally and formulate realistic verbal responses.

When the source of the anger is not readily accessible, a helpful strategy for expression is the use of an "anger stick." Take a newspaper apart and pile a sheet for each thing about which you're angry. State your emotion with every sheet you stack. For example, "I am angry because John was inconsiderate. I'm mad because he does this to everyone. It's irritating that he blows the Christian witness for all of us," etc. After all the sheets are stacked up, roll them tightly together and pound your anger stick on a very strong tree. This physical expression can take your fight away and leave you ready to talk out the problem with John.

Anger can also motivate us for pro-social action. When we see politicians misusing public funds, communities mistreating their minorities, or Christian leaders misrepresenting our Lord, it should make us mad. That anger can be a potent force in mobilizing us to remedy these abuses. Our energies might be directed to the voting booth or campaign trail. Perhaps we become mad enough to aid a victim personally or petition for change. We may need to confront a wayward Christian or lobby for action in our denomination. Anger so directed can be very constructive.

Forgive and Forget
After anger is detected, expressed, and acted on, we are left with only one more step for resolution. We must forgive. Forgiveness is a tall order and it may not be an appealing one. However, this process is akin to pulling a great fish into the fishing boat. The anger may have fought for its life while it was on the line, but it loses all its leverage when it is pulled from the sea into the boat of forgiveness. Forgiven offenses leave no bait on the hook for further struggles.

We have a divine precedent for forgiveness in God's actions toward us through Christ. Jesus taught His disciples to forgive even repeated offenses, and God demonstrates His willingness to wipe the slate clean each time we bring our sins to Him in confession. God's forgiveness releases us from guilt and brings us into fellowship with Him with the accompanying feeling of acceptance. When we forgive another, we bury our anger for good. This invites restored relationships and a focus on a bright future instead of on the dismal past.

Forgiveness is most difficult when the offense shows blatant disregard for others or when people in power abuse those in subjection to them. Such is the case when a drunken driver runs over an innocent victim, or when a husband beats his wife. In these cases anger is usually intense and forgiveness comes slowly. Human efforts at forgiveness may be ineffective because of the gravity of the offense, and divine assistance must be petitioned.

Karen was a thirty-five-year-old wife and mother who consulted me because she was deeply depressed. Investigation of her early adolescent years revealed a sickening pattern of physically abusive and incestuous activities by Karen's alcoholic father. She screamed how she hated her father for his wickedness and blamed him for her depression and her sexual difficulties with her husband.

We worked for a number of months on Karen's anger, and she learned to express it freely as she reviewed her life. Karen opened a subsequent session with the question, "Now that I've expressed all of my anger, what should I do next?" She was surprised to hear me mention forgiveness, because I had been such a strong ally in joining her and God in condemning her father's perverted and abusive activities. She asked, "How can you suggest that he deserves to be forgiven?" I replied, "*He* doesn't deserve to be forgiven, but *you* deserve to be released from your anger." I reasoned with Karen that her father had poisoned over twenty years of her life; it would be a tragedy for him to ruin the remainder of it.

I worked with Karen on releasing her father's behaviors to God and forgiving her father for her own sake and God's sake. The process was a difficult one because there was so much indignation. But finally she succeeded and found a total release. This kind of forgiveness can come only from a divine source, and that source is available to all of us to complete our anger transactions.

NINE

"Why are you downcast, O my soul?
Why so disturbed within me?"
Psalm 52:5

Get Back Up

A prominent religious leader who had seen the power of God evidenced mightily in his ministry took inventory of himself and reported the following symptoms: He was in great fear of those who opposed his ministry, and tried to "hide out" so they couldn't find him. This caused him to withdraw almost totally from others and produced a lonely persuasion that no one cared about him or shared his concerns. His physical health suffered as he quit eating regularly and deprived himself of sleep. As his dejection grew, he began to wonder about God's concern for him as well. He forgot God's previous and undeniable empowering of his ministry and instead focused on his current discouraging plight. As his hope sank, so did his willingness to live. He found himself praying for God to take him home.

You don't have to be a psychologist to know that he was suffering from depression. However, you might be surprised to learn the man's identity—the Prophet Elijah. Fortunately, he recovered from his depression, performed many more miraculous works for the Lord, and was translated directly to heaven without dying (1 Kings 19).

Depression is the common cold of psychology, in that it brings more people into psychotherapy than any other malady. We all feel mildly depressed periodically, but severe or prolonged depression can be very debilitating. It is estimated that twelve percent of the males and twenty percent of the females in the United States will experience a major depressive episode in their lifetimes. Depression will be severe enough to require hospitalization for about three percent of the males and six percent of the females. At any moment, about one and one-half million Americans are in professional treatment for depression, leaving anywhere from three to five times that many who need to be in treatment but are not. It is a nondiscriminatory illness, affecting persons from all socioeconomic groups. It has even been observed in other species like dogs and monkeys.[8]

The Symptoms

As you might expect of an ailment which is so prevalent, depression has many symptoms. The most prominent one is that terrible feeling of being sad and blue. A once-popular song likened the emotion to that experienced on rainy days and Mondays. When we're depressed, life just seems gloomier and the forecast promises no fair weather.

Another common symptom is the loss of interest in usual activities. Things that used to seem pleasurable now look dull. Brenda doesn't want to paint anymore for relaxation. Sam begins to dread the church activities which once highlighted his weekend. Frances loses her sexual drive. Depressed people can't seem to motivate themselves.

Most people who are depressed report sleep disturbances. We have all had the experience of lying awake at night thinking about something that went wrong during the day. People struggling with deep depression may not be able to get to sleep at all. Still others awaken and have difficulty falling back to sleep. This insomnia is extremely frustrating since the depressed person is usually worn-out physically and emotionally. Many complain that morning is the worst time of their day. A less common symptom is hypersomnia—sleeping much more than usual. For these people sleep acts as a defense against a depressing reality.

Depression also affects eating habits. When people are mildly depressed, they may eat more, since eating is an enjoyable activity which can temporarily rescue them from low feelings. But more often, depression causes people to lose their appetite—a very painful way to lose weight.

A complaint I hear from all of my depressed patients is that they are fatigued. Depression saps their energy and makes them tired even when they have not exerted themselves physically. Everything they do seems like a tremendous chore. Their children can't understand why they don't want to taxi them to the ball game, and their spouses wonder why they don't get off the couch and do something fun. Depressed persons' inability to snap out of their moods and jump back into life may make others doubt the sincerity of their efforts and drive them away. This is tragic because during these down times depressed people need others even more than usual.

As if that isn't enough, depression also impairs thinking. It's hard to concentrate and almost impossible to make a decision. Every thought seems to pass through the mind in slow motion. Depressed people are more forgetful and feel frustrated when they can't retain their thoughts. Students who are depressed about their borderline grades usually have great difficulty studying or remembering material for the final exam.

Perhaps the worst symptom of depression is the feeling of self-doubt and worthlessness that it generates. Depressed people are quite adept at identifying their personal weaknesses, exaggerating these failures, and unearthing a mountain of evidence conclusively proving their ineptitude. This negative focus permeates everything and, if prolonged, leads to hopelessness. The patriarch Job, who was confronted with family, material, and physical losses in a matter of days, expressed this symptom aptly: "My eyes will never see happiness again" (Job 7:7).

Hopelessness fosters the most serious threat of all from depression—suicide. The World Health Organization estimates that yearly 365,000 people take their own lives. In the United States there is one suicide attempt every sixty seconds and one completed suicide every seventeen and one-half minutes. This is the second leading cause of death among adolescents—every day eighteen American teenagers kill themselves.

The statistics are staggering, but the individual stories are heartwrenching. A sixty-year-old man shoots himself after a bout with depression over his nonproductivity at work. A thirty-five-year-old mother swallows every pill in the medicine chest because she can't seem to enjoy caring for her children. A seventeen-year-old girl hangs herself in the washroom of a drive-in after fighting with her boyfriend. Every incident is tragic and leaves a wake of human suffering for surviving family and friends.

The Sources

Colleen was a forty-five-year-old mother of two teenage sons. She and her husband began a small business which blossomed into a lucrative career for both of them. She confided in me that they were making money hand over fist. She was very active in her local church, and her family was a major contributor to the church's ministry.

But there was a snafu—Colleen felt unhappy. She was often tired and lost her motivation to put time into the business. It was difficult for her to fall asleep at night and she didn't have much of an appetite. She complained, "Everything I have to do is a chore and I don't feel I'm doing a good job at anything anymore."

Colleen was obviously depressed, but the reason was not clear. She reported comfort in her relationship with God. Her family was very supportive of her, and her husband was her most ardent encourager. She was in good health, and the doctor who referred her to me could find no physical reason for her symptoms. Since she had plenty of money, finances couldn't be the problem. Or could they?

After several weeks of therapy, I noticed a distinct drop in Colleen's mood whenever she mentioned money. Investigation of this issue unearthed the source of her depression.

Colleen had grown up in a family which was long on love but very short on cash. She had felt loved for who she was. Her newfound wealth changed her perceptions. Now she always wondered why others befriended her. Did they like her or her money? Money—a lot of it—was the source of her depression. Once recognized, Colleen learned ways to check out her perceptions and lift her spirits.

Although this example is a bit unusual, it demonstrates that almost anything is a potential source of depression. Too little money would have been quickly identified as the source, but too much was overlooked. Recognizing the source of depression can help us understand our feelings; it can also interrupt the downward spiral of low spirits to withdrawal. Depression can be classified into two categories—those which are internally caused (endogenous depression) and those which are reactions to environmental events (exogenous depression). Let's look at both.

• Endogenous depression. Some cases of depression strike with no apparent cause. The devoted minister who is incapacitated by low spirits, the popular adolescent who suddenly becomes distraught, and the successful businesswoman who can't motivate herself to go to work—these are difficult for us to understand. Everything in their lives seems to be going right and yet they feel blue. Before insisting that these people must have carefully camouflaged problems or that they are undoubtedly engaged in some secret, sinful behavior pattern, we need to consider that there might be a biological basis for their depression.

Most of us recognize how physical illnesses deplete our energy and lower our moods. It makes sense that depression commonly accompanies serious diseases; yet even less formidable maladies such as influenza may trigger depressed feelings as well. Sometimes physical conditions not apparent to others, such as hypothyroidism, low blood sugar, or premenstrual tension may stimulate our down feelings.

Researchers have discovered some evidence for hereditary links to depression. Studies of families, twins, and adoptions suggest that depression may have a genetic component.[9] But this evidence is far from conclusive and it is probably more accurate to say that our genetic makeup may provide a predisposition to depression, but many other factors must come into play for it to develop fully.

Some chemical changes in the body may also contribute to low moods. In their quest to identify biological reasons for depression, researchers have been particularly interested in the substances which transmit nerve impulses from neuron to neuron (neurotransmitters). In chemical analyses of the blood of depressed persons, deficiencies of the neurotransmitters noradrenaline, secrotonin, and dopamine have been found. Interestingly, excessive stress is known to deplete these substances; perhaps this explains some of the depression that bogs us down when our lives become very harried.[10] Of course, it is hard to say whether these chemical deficiencies actually precipitate the depression or if they are merely an effect of the low-mood state.

The biblical account of King Saul seems to indicate unexplained bouts with depression. During Saul's low moods, David was called in to cheer his ruler by playing soothing music on the harp. This remedy would work at times, but at other times the king would become violent. Perhaps he suffered from biochemical abnormalities which fostered this unpredictability. We can never be certain about this ancient ruler, but we cannot afford to overlook the possible physical causes for our feelings. When we become depressed for any significant length of time without a recognized environmental cause, a checkup by the physician is clearly in order.

● Exogenous depression. It is much more common to find the source of depressive moods in the events surrounding us. Depression often accompanies losses. When someone close to us dies, we may feel down in the dumps or blue. This happened to Jesus' followers after His crucifixion. Luke records Jesus' encounter on the road to Emmaus with two of His disciples and describes them as having downcast faces. They felt depressed until the truth of the Resurrection was made apparent to them. King David's grief over the terminal illness of his infant son is recorded in 2 Samuel 12. God took this boy as a consequence of David's sins of adultery and murder. David refused food, lay on the ground for extended periods, and wept constantly in response to God's decision.

Stress is a very real source of depression. When we are overtaxed and the pressure seems unrelenting, our spirits tend to sink. Financial reversals, relationship ruptures, and work overload often push people beyond their coping capacity and depression quickly ensues. The major factor that determines whether stress will lead to depression appears to be one's sense of control in the throes of the stressor. If Fred is greeted at work with an unexpected notice that his plant is closing in sixty days, he will undoubtedly experience a good deal of stress. However, if he recognizes his spiritual resources, has a financial reserve, has been considering another position anyway, and has a supportive family, chances are he will feel some control over his situation and the stress will be handled adequately. If Fred catastrophizes that he is headed for the poorhouse, feels helpless to survive the closing, and recognizes no options for future employment, the stress will probably extend into a depressive episode.

The above illustration points to the critical role which thinking plays in depression. Irrational, distorted, or negative thinking patterns usher a deflated mood to the center of one's being. Psychologists have identified some dysfunctional thought processes which are especially prevalent in depressed people. Negative exaggeration is one culprit. This occurs when Sally reasons that her afternoon presentation must have been horrible since the client did not give her a contract immediately. Then she may overgeneralize and tell herself that no one will ever buy from her and that it is foolish to persist in her career. She may compare herself unfavorably to Bob, who landed an account today, and magnify every personal fault she ever observed in herself. This river of negative thinking is almost certain to empty into a sea of depression.

The link between anger and depression was suggested many years ago by Freudian psychologists. They believed that depression is caused by unconscious aggressive impulses which are in danger of being revealed to the conscious mind. Since this threatens the person, the aggression is turned inward and no outward expression of anger occurs. The aggression is experienced as depression.

Depression may follow close on the heels of a very invigorating experience. Many doctors who finally finish their grueling graduate study become depressed after graduation. A couple who scrapes to purchase the house of their dreams will often move in and experience the doldrums of buyer's remorse. Mothers who anticipate bringing a precious new life into the world sometimes find themselves suffering from postpartum depression after delivery.

The dips that follow emotional highs are confusing and usually take us by surprise. Elijah's depression, described earlier in this chapter, is a case in point. We might expect his mental condition to have arisen from a prolonged period of inefficiency in his ministry and a failure to see God's hand upon his work. Just the opposite was true. The event which immediately preceded his depressive episode was Elijah's contest with the prophets of Baal on Mount Carmel, where the Lord evidenced His superiority mightily through His servant in front of the entire nation of Israel.

The Prophet Jonah also experienced significant depression after preaching one of the greatest revivals in recorded history. His proclamation of God's message to the ancient Ninevites resulted in repentance by the entire population and stayed God's plans for their destruction. But Jonah's request to God to "take away my life, for it is better for me to die than to live" (Jonah 4:3) and his subsequent sulking about God's goodness were depressive symptoms occasioned by his selfishness. Jonah did not want Nineveh spared, and it took divine transportation via a whale to produce the prophet for his speaking engagement in the first place.

Selfishness often results in low spirits as we become so caught up in our own concerns that we fail to recognize the needs of others. Some people become childish, like King Ahab who pouted and refused to eat because Naboth refused to sell his vineyard. Others withdraw silently, brooding over their disappointed expectations and lamenting their unfortunate fate. We can't be happy while selfishly pursuing our own goals to the exclusion of others.

Given the multitude of avenues by which depression can infect our moods, it is no wonder these symptoms are so prevalent. Whether these feelings seep in through biochemical reactions in the body or travel the well-worn road of irrational ideas, they are a force we must all reckon with from time to time. Recognizing the source of a depression may provide a framework for self-understanding and ready us to climb out of the emotional pit.

The Solutions
The reality of God's presence is reassuring during any emotional upheaval, but it seems particularly so when we are depressed. Unfortunately, our perception is often one of both Divine and human abandonment. The foundational rung on the ladder to recovery is assurance of God's steadfastness. Paul asserted this fact mightily in his Epistle to the Romans by numbering heights and depths along with all other elements which are powerless to separate us from the love of God. We must focus on this immutable presence of God to get back up again.

It is also imperative that we remain hopeful of recovery. Depression thrives on pessimism, and the prospect of unending sadness always accompanies bouts with the blues. Deficiency of hope cripples us because it paralyzes our will to take any action. Hopelessness must be short-circuited, and a recognition of God's assistance is the most potent circuit breaker available.

King David demonstrated this repeatedly in the gripping descriptions of his own emotional struggles. For instance, in Psalm 69 David vividly likened his depression to being engulfed by deep waters, enclosed in a pit and entrapped in the mire. Yet he prayed, "I am in pain and distress; may Your salvation, O God, protect me" (v. 29), and he ended his hymn with verses of praise. Likewise in Psalms 42 and 43 he repeats these questions three times along with the solution: "Why are you downcast, O my soul? Why so disturbed within me? Put your hope in God, for I will yet praise Him, my Saviour and my God." We cannot afford to ignore our divine Source of hope.

The next step on the road to recovery is sharing your feelings with concerned others. Depression is a heavy burden to carry alone; putting on a happy face will not eliminate the problem. Admit your struggles and talk them through with people who will listen and accept you in your honesty. Openness about their feelings, even to the point of expressing their questions about wanting to live, was a common feature of each of the biblical characters described in this chapter. This openness is especially appropriate when grieving a loss or confronting a serious illness.

Unfortunately, expression of feeling is not by itself usually sufficient to ward off depression; it must be accompanied by attitude and behavior change. In fact, people who only talk bout their troubles but take no action to solve them tend to feel even more depressed. And those who associate with depressed people also tire quickly of their never-ending sad stories. I have often observed my depressed patients resist positive action and thus erode their social support networks. They don't realize how depressing communication drives friends away.

The ultimate treatment strategy is attitude change, but it is helped along considerably by behavior modification. It takes concerted action to free ourselves from the downhill slide of depression. We must pay attention to our physical needs and meet them when appropriate. God initially dealt with Elijah's depression by feeding him. We need to get back to a proper diet, sleep schedule, and activity level and break the withdrawal cycle by reinitiating social activities and church attendance. Some research suggests that vigorous physical activity, such as running, is effective in treating depression.[11] Exercise consumes stress products and releases chemicals called endorphins in our brains. This biologically lifts our mood. We can't afford to wait until we feel like doing something because these feelings may only result from positive movement.

Besides improving our health, these actions also better our attitude. They show us we still have the power to change ourselves. They restore some of our confidence and feelings of self-control. They also distract us from self-defeating thoughts and move us in a positive direction.

The next rung on the ladder to recovery is the critical issue of attitude change. As was discussed thoroughly in chapter 6, our negative feelings are never far away from our negative thoughts. Cognitive restructuring is widely used by psychologists to treat depression, but professional counselors were not the first to discover the efficiency of thought modification. In response to Elijah's exaggeration that he was the only person left in Israel who worshiped Jehovah, God enlightened His prophet that 7,000 of his countrymen were also devout believers. When Moses reached the end of his rope, assuring himself that things would never get better, and asking God to take his life, the Almighty's answer was to show His servant a way to release the pressure by delegating many duties to a staff of seventy elders. As God changed the thinking of these Old Testament saints, their outlook changed.

The strategy works equally well today. Marsha is typical of many depressed persons who consult me. She was in her mid-twenties and married to a man she described as a fine husband. But Marsha complained that she often felt blue. No physical reason for her low mood could be found, so we began investigating her life circumstances and thought patterns. It soon became evident that Marsha was very self-critical. She detected every conceivable personal fault, from her occasionally wandering mind during devotions and prayer to the one minuscule flaw in her otherwise clear complexion. As she repeatedly reminded herself of her defects, her joy waned. Her husband and others who would never fault her for these tiny blemishes found themselves repelled from Marsha because of her depression. She reported to me that they said she was not much fun anymore. Thus, her depression deepened.

Marsha's treatment was almost totally in the thinking realm. Indeed, the faults she observed were common to everyone and not amenable to change. After reasserting her hope in the Lord, we began bushwhacking her hyper-critical self-statements with the machete of rational thoughts. She came to recognize her exaggerations and overgeneralizations, and then learned to dispute and replace them with more realistic ideas. (Refer to chapter 6 for the details of this process.) Over time her mood improved and her exuberance returned.

We must never underestimate the value of checking our thinking when our emotions begin to dip. "Poor me" attitudes, selfishness, perfectionistic thinking, and exaggeration foster depression and respond when treated by rational thought replacement.

In cases of endogenous depression and very intense or extended depression, medication may be necessary to lift one's mood. Lithium salt is effective in treating some persons who fluctuate between very excitable and very depressed moods. Tricyclic antidepressants and monoamine oxidase inhibitors are also prescribed frequently for persons with severe depressions. These medications may lift one's spirits enough to get him started on the ladder to recovery. They must be prescribed by a physician and are almost always used in conjunction with psychotherapy.

In every phase of our dealings with depression, we should be aware of the power available from others to enhance our progress. God's provision of these people to love, listen and share our burdens offers us great comfort. It was not coincidental that the same chapter of 1 Kings which describes Elijah's struggles also records God's provision of Elisha to His weary prophet—a companion who remained with Elijah for the rest of his life.

SECTION 4

People—you can't live with them and you can't live without them. However, living with or without others is not our choice. We're in a world with five billion people and isolation is not possible. Our real choice comes down to who we will relate to and how we will do it.

Choosing persons with whom to associate on a regular basis is a delicate business. We have the example of Jesus, who regularly associated with persons of questionable character (prostitutes, tax collectors, etc.), and His suggestion that such wide association was to be expected. "It is not the healthy who need a doctor, but the sick. I have not come to call the righteous but sinners to repentance" (Luke 5:31-32).

However, Paul warned, "Do not be misled: Bad company corrupts good character" (1 Corinthians 15:33), recognizing that we tend to adopt the behaviors and attitudes of those with whom we spend our time. Whenever we immerse ourselves in associations with people who are not uplifting, we are prone to adopt many of their actions and attitudes. Being in the world but not of it has presented dilemmas for Christians throughout the ages.

The other aspect of the interpersonal equation is how we will relate to those with whom we choose to associate. The Apostle Paul devoted maximum attention to this topic, repeatedly imploring believers to accept one another, bear each other's burdens, and live in harmony together. Our effectiveness in interpersonal contact, as well as the nourishment we receive from others, is directly propor-

tional to the relational skills we master and implement.

Strategies for opening channels of communication are presented in chapter 10; techniques useful in resolving conflicts with cooperative and uncooperative persons are explained in chapter 11.

TEN

*"A word aptly spoken is like apples of
gold in settings of silver."
Proverbs 25:11*

Can We Talk?

In *Pygmalion,* playwright George Bernard Shaw unfolds
the delightful tale of Elisa Doolittle's transformation from a
cockney flower peddler to a grand lady thought to be roy-
alty. Her metamorphosis was accomplished under the tute-
lage of linguist Henry Higgins, who hounded her mercilessly until she learned to speak perfect English and then fell
in love with his creation. Elisa *became* a different person
when she learned to *communicate* as a different person.
This training dramatically changed the quality of her life.

The Morgan family was in crisis when they met me in my
office. Fifteen-year-old Jack had been arrested for shoplift-
ing. He sat sullenly between his father and twelve-year-old
sister, Rita, while Mrs. Morgan thoroughly detailed every
incident of her son's life. While Mother rambled on, Jack
rolled his eyes with each new disclosure. Meanwhile, Rita
vied for Mr. Morgan's attention by cleverly entangling her
arm in her seat back and feigning inability to free herself.
These actions were communicating volumes to me but very
little to my clients. Since no one dared to compete for
speaking time with Mrs. Morgan, they all employed creative
ways to communicate with one another. Rita received attention through her ineptness. Mr. Morgan was the dutiful
sounding board for his wife and troubleshooter for the

kids. Jack resorted to desperate means to let her know that he needed attention. As usual, Mom just talked her way through everything, oblivious to her family's real needs.

The Morgans were caught in a tangled communication web, and it was no small chore to help them untangle themselves. However, as with Elisa Doolittle, when the Morgans learned to communicate properly, their quality of life improved appreciably.

The Necessity of Good Communication

Communication impacts every aspect of our lives. The believer's direct access to God through prayer is a major distinctive of Protestant Christianity. An open line of vertical communication to God is vital for spiritual growth and fulfillment.

Likewise, horizontal channels of open communication with others are a biblical mandate. As the poet John Donne paraphrased the Apostle Paul, "No man is an island." Jesus stressed the importance of positive interpersonal relationships and modeled clear communication to persons from all stations of life. The epistles are replete with exhortations to connect regularly with the family of believers. God intended for His children to communicate well.

Unfortunately, we possess quite a penchant for miscommunication. The comedy which ensues from verbal misunderstandings is entertaining at the theater or on the screen. Few can resist smiling at Abbott and Costello's "Who's on First?" routine or the royal cases of mistaken identity in a Shakespearean comedy. However, personal experiences of miscommunication are rarely amusing.

A breakdown in communication tends to distance people from one another. The generations following the flood had a thriving civilization and decided to build a tower to solidify their unity. God responded to their plan by confusing their languages, so that friends and coworkers could no longer understand each other. They deserted the Tower of Babel and dispersed, settling with others who spoke their own language.

But even before God confused languages at Babel, humans had difficulty communicating clearly. Immediately after Adam and Eve first sinned, their communication style underwent radical changes. Whereas before they walked openly with God, disclosing everything to Him, Genesis 3 records how they now hid from God. Even when God approached Adam with the direct question, "Have you eaten from the tree that I commanded you not to eat from?" Adam answered evasively, implicating his wife as the culprit. Thus, with original sin came the first remnants of *denial* and *projection*—defensive mechanisms which still today thwart interpersonal openness and hinder communication.

In Genesis 4 we read of Cain's lie, as he told God he knew nothing about his murdered brother. And by the time of Noah, people were so wicked that God destroyed all but eight of them. Unfortunately, miscommunication survived the flood.

Now humans are well adapted to all of these communication ills and they have developed many more—slander, blasphemy, the half-truth, withdrawal, and endless chatter, to name a few. Positive communication demands skill and practice. The balance of this chapter deals with these skills.

Avoid Excesses

Talk does not necessarily guarantee communication. Some persons talk endlessly without saying anything. Nonstop talking is usually associated with low intelligence. As the scarecrow in *The Wizard of Oz* explains to Dorothy when she asks how he can talk without a brain, "Some people without brains do an awful lot of talking." Solomon associates verbosity with unrighteousness: "When words are many, sin is not absent" (Proverbs 10:19). So when we think we've said aplenty, plenty of people will be happy if we say no more.

We can be excessive in the opposite direction as well. Some people withdraw almost to complete silence. Our fifth-grade teacher may have richly rewarded this excess, but it does little to enhance our adult relationships. Many women complain to me in marriage counseling that their husbands never talk to them. I've watched some of these men cling steadfastly to their silence even when their wives plead for any intelligible utterance. How tragic to withhold words of love and encouragement. Solomon likens pleasant words to a honeycomb "sweet to the soul and healing to the bones," and a word aptly spoken to "apples of gold in settings of silver" (Proverbs 16:24; 25:11). Excessive silence deprives our families and friends of these vital resources.

We should also avoid excesses in harmful categories of talking. One complaint high on this list is nagging. Those considerate reminders that we so caringly present to others take on a very different meaning when they are repeated. Most adolescents I see in psychotherapy complain that their parents nag them to nausea. The parents usually see their reminders in a very different light. No one likes to be nagged. It signals disrespect and lack of confidence that one is responsible. Nagging is also very draining. Judges 16 describes Delilah's constant nagging of Samson to reveal the source of his strength as "vexing him sore unto death" (KJV), and it eventually wore Samson down with tragic consequences. All of us have felt like Samson—we just want to turn off the faucet. Usually the easiest way to do this is to avoid the nagger.

Perhaps the most destructive and most common excess is gossip. In Scripture this behavior is denounced in very stern language. Gossip is insidious because it preys so cunningly on our natural curiosity and often begins as a valid inquiry into the well-being of others. However, when we repeat the material indiscriminantly, we involve ourselves in potential damage to the targeted person—damage which may be multiplied many times over. One safe rule for gauging your talk about others: If your contribution is not part of the solution, it's part of the problem. There's no need to fuel the local rumor mill.

Opening a Clear Channel

Periodically I will take my two daughters, ages five and eight, for a special outing. I inevitably end up at the frozen yogurt parlor discussing issues as diverse as which waffle cone is most flavorful to how stocks involve one in the ownership of a company. Of course most of the communication is devoted to personal issues, and I find each occasion rewarding and enlightening.

I learn more about clear communication from these outings than from any graduate course. The children are honest, respond enthusiastically to attention, and wait patiently for my answers. They ask straightforward questions and are sincere when they tell me that my answers are clear or confusing. My girls have taught me how to avoid phoniness and to communicate frankly.

Functional communication with our children or with anyone else demands an attitude of openness from us. It involves listening in a way that is apparent to our partner. It also requires the selection of appropriate words and subsequent actions which make those words believable. Good communication takes some effort!

• Our attitudes. I once saw a cartoon depicting a wise marriage counselor summing up his findings to a couple who were sneering at each other. The gist of his diagnosis was, "The problem is definitely communication. Now you'll have to find a way to *avoid* it." Although the cartoon was meant to be humorous, the pronouncement may sometimes seem accurate. Some people communicate very clearly, but still have legions of interpersonal problems. This is because they are plainly broadcasting sentiments such as, "I hate you," or "I think you're a jerk." Their clarity worsens their relationship problems.

The place to begin any discussion of communication techniques is not with what to say, but rather with our attitudes toward others. As Jesus reminded us, "Out of the overflow of (a person's) heart his mouth speaks" (Luke 6:45). A positive attitude toward others will aid communication because good will enhances any verbal expressions.

Likewise, unfriendly feelings are evident, regardless of our words, since most of us are very poor actors on the interpersonal stage. Judas' kiss and greeting of Jesus as "Rabbi" hardly camouflaged his betrayal of the Lord.

The first principle of good communication is an attitude of acceptance and respect for the other person. This is not to say that we accept or respect every position he takes. Any parent will quickly recognize the difference. My daughters sometimes determine that their disagreements are best adjudicated by a verbal and physical assault on each other. I abhor this behavior and must intervene at times to restore order to the household. Because I love my children, I express my dislike for their actions while affirming my respect for them as persons. This is essential if I expect to keep communication channels open with them.

The Apostle Paul wrote extensively on the importance of acceptance, especially among members of the body of Christ. He issued the imperative, "Accept one another, then, just as Christ accepted you, in order to bring praise to God" (Romans 15:7). We are to bear with one another in love.

• Listening. We would be very concerned if a jury returned a verdict against us for a criminal charge before giving us a chance to answer the charges. We expect to gain a hearing for our evidence before decisions affecting our freedom are made. Likewise, we don't want the physician to write a prescription for us until she listens to our health complaints. We expect others to listen to us before they impact our lives.

Yet in our daily contacts, many of us routinely violate this principle. We say no to our children's requests before hearing their reasoning. We advise our spouses on how to deal with their supervisors without first listening to their complaints or to the solutions they have already attempted. In an effort to offer spiritual encouragement, we recite a Bible verse to a fellow parishioner without first giving him the benefit of sharing his struggles. It's just hard for us to listen.

An essential of good communication is following James' directive to "be quick to listen and slow to speak" (James 1:19). We are often so very busy with our own projects and struggles that we have little time to process the cares and concerns of others. When we take the time to move into the world of others, we gain their perspectives; and endear ourselves to them. We may even learn something new!

Solomon distinguished between the folly and shame of answering before listening and the wisdom of seeking out knowledge (Proverbs 18:13, 15). The key ingredient in listening is maintaining a tight hold on our tongues. Repeatedly Solomon associated understanding with this ability, and foolishness, calamity, and lack of judgment with speaking in haste. I believe this is one reason so many people ascribe a good deal of intelligence to their pets. A dumb animal sits contentedly while being petted and listens attentively to our every word without interrupting.

Besides keeping our tongues in check, we demonstrate active listening by facing those who talk to us, maintaining good eye contact, and avoiding distractions. Eye contact is probably the most critical evidence of listening. It is hard to convince our spouses that we want to hear their news when we're watching the television or looking out the window. Our children will demand our "listening eyes" with requests to "Watch me, Daddy!" or by jumping in our laps. When we favor others with our full physical attention, they are much more willing to share their joys as well as their sorrows.

One caution in listening is to avoid "hearing" too much. Ecclesiastes 7:21-22 warns, "Do not pay attention to every word people say, or you may hear your servant cursing you—for you know in your heart that many times you yourself have cursed others." Many of us adeptly hear unfortunate communications from others and log them permanently in our memory banks with immediate recall capability. Often these criticisms are spoken in haste or anger and do not represent the real sentiments of the speaker. Be willing to forgive a personal affront and press your brain's delete button to erase it from storage after you offer forgiveness. I see so many couples in psychotherapy who are great historians, able to describe in vivid detail every angry word their spouses have ever uttered. Sometimes forgetfulness is a wonderful convenience, especially when mixed with a sense of humor.

• Responding. With attitudes in an acceptance mode and ears fine-tuned for listening, it's finally time to say something ourselves. But even now communication is not assured. It is our responsibility to convey our message in a manner understandable to others. It's not always enough merely to use correct grammar and excellent pronunciation. Until others understand the sense we are trying to make, we have not communicated.

This became very clear to me the summer I graduated from college. Before entering graduate school in the fall, I worked at various jobs to earn tuition money. One of them was a seven-week stint as a laborer in a large fixture company. The low wage attracted many transient workers, and I was assigned to a department that was predominantly Spanish-speaking. I enjoyed the experience immensely as we discovered creative nonverbal ways to communicate, and I learned many Spanish words.

However, our foreman did not share my enthusiasm. Mr. Albertson barked orders in English at everyone, expecting immediate compliance with his directives. A bilingual employee usually rescued his Spanish-speaking friends from confusion. But one day he was absent and Mr. Albertson needed a table moved. He approached Fernando from Argentina and commanded, "Move the table over there." Fernando gave a puzzled look and said something in Spanish. Mr. Albertson repeated his desire, "Move the table over there." Fernando looked even more confused, so Mr. Albertson attempted to clarify his wishes by stating more slowly and emphatically, "MOVE! THE! TABLE! OVER! THERE!" The table might never have been moved had I not intervened with some simple sign language and pointing.

The illustration seems humorous as I reflect on it now,

but Fernando and Jack Albertson never did see anything funny about it. No one enjoys being stranded in a miscommunication. Yet we often become so cemented in the expressions we use that our meaning is never conveyed. It's our responsibility to express ourselves so that our audience understands what we're saying. This is especially important when we talk with children.

As good communicators, we demonstrate to others that we have listened to them before offering our own point of view. We accomplish this by a simple and concise restatement of the gist of what we've heard. To a friend who describes a boating adventure to us, we might first say, "Your weekend on the water sounds very exciting." *Then* we could recount highlights of an outing on the river we enjoyed. The boss may invite us into her office and present a list of positive and negative observations about our performance. Instead of launching into a defense of our proposed weaknesses, we might augment our remarks with a concise restatement of our boss' findings. "So you're pleased with my organization of the department, the new employees hired, and the new product ideas. However, you perceive problems in my marketing strategy and computer selections. I'd like to share my frustrations in our sales with you." A simple reflection of what we've heard proves that we've listened and invites our listeners to afford us the same courtesy.

In conversations with family members or close associates, feelings are often shared. This is encouraging since communicating on the emotional level usually reflects a positive relationship. Here especially, a restatement of the emotion our partner has shared greatly strengthens the interpersonal bond. We can accomplish this easily by declaring, "You feel happy, sad, angry, frustrated, down, confused" (or any other appropriate feeling word).

Communication breakdowns frequently occur when we ignore our partner's feelings and respond only to the facts presented. Our spouse may tell us, "I don't know what to do with Billy. He sits in front of his books all afternoon, but hardly completes any of his homework. Then he wants to watch television after supper." The typical response begins, "Why don't you. . . ." A better response begins, "I can see you're really frustrated with Billy. . . ." Our spouse wants to be heard as much as she desires our child-training advice. Demonstrating that we've listened gives us permission to make suggestions. We must also be careful never to deny our partner's feelings no matter how different they are from our own or how silly they seem. Replace, "You shouldn't feel angry" with "You feel angry, but I don't understand why."

Good communicators are also thoughtful in their responses. This may seem obvious, but it takes little personal reflection to remember our violations of this principle. We think, "If I had only thought before I said that about Gene. That's her father-in-law, for goodness sakes." Thoughtfulness is a miracle cure for foot-in-mouth disease. Proverbs 15:28 puts it succinctly: "The heart of the righteous weighs its answers." Most of us could benefit from a good daily dose of this preventive medicine.

A healthy way to communicate our thoughtfulness is through employing tact whenever we speak. Paul advised, "Let your conversation be always full of grace, seasoned with salt, so that you may know how to answer everyone" (Colossians 4:6). In this context he was describing evangelism, and it is interesting to see how Paul practiced this principle in his own ministry. In Acts 17 Paul was brought before the people of Athens to present his ideas. He was greatly distressed by all the idols he saw in the city; but instead of condemning his audience for their paganism, he commended them for their religiosity and brought their attention to an idol bearing the inscription: TO AN UNKNOWN GOD. This arrested their attention and provided Paul with an audience engrossed in his proclamation of the Gospel. It's amazing how a little seasoning makes our communication more palatable.

We should also avoid the use of questions unless we need specific information. Many interrogative statements are used to convey our opinions, not to gather data from others. "Didn't I tell you that would happen?" and "Can't you ever get it right?" are prime examples. A person would look as foolish when answering these questions as we sound condescending when asking them. The rule of thumb maintains that we should never ask a question in conversation to which we already know the answer.

We should make statements of our questions. "Where have you been? Don't you know I'm hungry?" can be transformed into "I've been concerned about your absence and what we'll do for dinner." If we feel strongly, we can state our feelings strongly, but not in a rhetorical question. "I'm angry about your handling of this contract" is more direct and less demeaning than "Can't you even handle a simple contract?" Questions which demand no answer shut down communication and serve only to drive people away from us. And frankly, who can blame them?

Keep a positive focus. When we attack others or illuminate all their faults, we build barriers. It is much more helpful to focus on our desired expectations for positive actions than to malign others for their inadequacies or to predict future failure. I recently observed my wife accomplishing this masterfully when the movers were transporting our belongings into our new house. During the first few trips she watched the men and complimented them liberally for the care with which they handled our cargo. Then she periodically extolled their performance and conveyed her anticipation of a continued damage-free move. The movers felt respected and carried out their task with none of the damage to the house and furniture which we usually encounter. Her communications were neither phony nor manipulative. She believed in the movers' abilities to perform admirably and simply encouraged them to rise to their potential.

• Quitting. A final skill to enhance our responses is to know when to quit talking. We usually underestimate the percentage of time we talk in a transaction with another, and thus we are not aware how we monopolize conversations. Professors have a wonderful means to help counselors in training recognize their verbosity—the tape recorder. As I listen to tapes with the students I supervise, they often cringe at their long discourses—which they could shorten to a matter of seconds. Their concise statements are usually much more effective.

Most of us will never hear a recording of our daily conversations, but we can gauge our verbosity simply by watching the reactions of others. When people are becoming bored, they deny us steady eye contact and back away physically. We should use these cues to signal a conclusion to our speech. We don't have to know something about every topic. Sometimes our most appropriate response is silence. When asked a question about an unfamiliar topic, Abraham Lincoln replied, "As I have nothing to say, I will say nothing at all." This tactic can rescue us from great embarrassment as well. A common paraphrase of Proverbs 17:28 declares: It is better to be thought a fool and remain silent than to speak and remove all doubt.

In *Pygmalion* George Bernard Shaw said that the British and Americans were two peoples separated by a common language. The same is too often true about us as we raise miscommunication to an art form. Conveyance of meaning demands observation of proven skills and their practice on a continual basis. In this way we can communicate through our common language and heal our interpersonal ruptures.

ELEVEN

*"Each of you must put off falsehood and
speak truthfully to his neighbor, for we
are all members of one body."
Ephesians 4:25*

When Conflict Arises

Paul and Barnabas made a tremendous evangelistic team. The Book of Acts records how Barnabas initially brought Paul to the church at Antioch and worked together with him, discipling great numbers of people. They later embarked on missionary journeys throughout Asia Minor, preaching mightily, establishing churches, and enduring intense persecution. Together they appeared before the church council at Jerusalem and convinced these Jewish Christians to embrace Gentile converts wholeheartedly.

After returning to Antioch to disciple the church, Paul asked Barnabas to accompany him on another missionary venture to the towns they earlier visited. Barnabas agreed and proposed that John Mark accompany them. Paul balked at this suggestion, pointing out that John Mark started with them last time but deserted them. These two mighty leaders who had walked so closely together disagreed sharply about this matter and parted company as a result.

Conflict presents itself routinely in our lives. The first human offspring murdered his brother, and siblings have been in rivalry ever since. Protestant denominations interpret the Scriptures differently and doctrinal conflicts arise. Christians disagree in their views of politics, entertainment, and just about every other issue under the sun. Spouses don't see eye to eye either. I once had a college professor who declared that he had *never* argued with his wife, and after that I was suspect of everything else he ever said.

Jesus faced interpersonal conflict daily. If He wasn't being challenged by the religious establishment, He had to contend with His bickering disciples. Even the perfect Man was not exempt from these consequences of a very imperfect world.

When we step outside of Christendom, the extent of global strife is staggering. Recently, a CBS news correspondent estimated that 100 million people have been killed in over 100 wars during the twentieth century alone. Jews and Arabs engage in a struggle to death over their common homeland. Irish Protestants and Catholics perpetuate a centuries-old conflict over their rule. Communist and capitalist nations disagree on most issues. Conflict is so thoroughly entwined into the fabric of our world that any harmony seems surprising.

Given this bleak picture, the odds against avoiding conflict in our personal lives are astronomical. What are our options? We can become forceful exponents of our own opinions and win our arguments. We can withdraw when conflicts arise and thereby forfeit the battle without even firing a shot. Or we can learn strategies helpful in resolving conflict with others in such a manner that each party suffers as little as possible.

Winning at All Costs

Competition is a human characteristic that transcends cultures, but nowhere is it more pervasive than in the United States. Businesses compete for market shares. Politicians compete for representation rights. Even children compete in beauty contests. Everyone in our culture wants to be number one. Athletes and their fans never hold up two or three fingers to the TV camera. They display the prominent index finger symbolizing the pinnacle of success—being number one.

Coach Vince Lombardi had the motto: "Winning isn't everything; it's the only thing." When one adopts this philosophy, his interactions with others become aggressive. Like a defensive lineman trying to sack the opposing quarterback, he resorts to any method available to achieve his objective. That usually translates into bullying actions such as blaming, threatening, or accusing others. His voice is loud, his attitude is superior, and his emotion is anger. The aggressive person seeks his own will, regardless of the consequences to others. He lives by the dictum: I matter and you don't.

Fortunately, aggressive persons are in the minority. However, most of us can name one or two with whom we've had contact. We learn quickly to stay well away from these persons and follow Solomon's advice, "Do not envy a violent man, or choose any of his ways" (Proverbs 3:31). Thus, the aggressive person pays a steep interpersonal price for winning confrontations.

Some Christians adopt an aggressive style to defend their faith against those who embrace divergent viewpoints. They argue forcefully for their interpretations of Scripture and are scathing in their attacks on dissenters. They resort to name-calling when other believers hold political views that differ from their own or when a sister denomination enacts policies which they see as deviant. They will argue at the drop of a hat.

How effective are these tactics in resolving conflict? Proverbs 17:14 warns, "Starting a quarrel is like breaching a dam; so drop the matter before a dispute breaks out." Paul, who faced many opposing views in his ministry, wrote to Timothy:

> *Don't have anything to do with foolish and stupid arguments, because you know they produce quarrels. And the Lord's servant must not quarrel; instead, he must be kind to everyone, able to teach, not resentful. Those who oppose him he must gently instruct. (2 Timothy 2:23-25)*

Likewise he wrote to Titus, "Avoid foolish controversies and genealogies and arguments and quarrels about the law, because these are unprofitable and useless" (Titus 3:9). Aggressive words are called the mark of a fool by Solomon and entering someone else's quarrel is the pinnacle of foolishness. "Like one who seizes a dog by the ears is a passerby who meddles in a quarrel not his own" (Proverbs 26:17).

Aggressiveness is no way to solve a conflict. It drives people from us, settles nothing, and labels us as fools. This hardly qualifies as a viable strategy.

I'm a Doormat; Please Wipe Your Feet

Since aggression is discouraged in Scripture, the opposite behavior must be in order—we can be passive. Jesus Himself said to turn the other cheek, and everyone expects good Christians to be humble and submissive. There will be no conflicts to resolve if we give others their own way. Right?

In our culture many more people are passive than aggressive. Passive people are quiet or apologetic. They are indirect in their expressions so others often must guess what they want. They are very agreeable and avert confrontations whenever possible. They live by the dictum: I don't matter but you do.

Passive Christians go with the flow. They don't like to ruffle any feathers, so they keep their opinions to themselves unless they are sure their audience will agree with them. Unfortunately, they also keep their faith to themselves for fear that the religious issue might be uncomfortable to others. They blend in well with their environment.

Passive Christians abdicate many responsibilities of their position as ambassadors for Christ. This prevents them from impacting the world for Christ and greatly reduces their ability to add "salt and light" to a world in need of both.

Besides, passivity doesn't work. It may reduce a present conflict, but a lifestyle of this posture invites much more conflict. When one is passive, he trains others to mistreat

him, and their mistreatment of him will inevitably general-
ize to his mistreatment of others. He keeps quiet about his
perceptions of others and thus denies them an opportunity
to change and grow from his observations. He violates the
biblical directives to speak the truth in love and to express
himself honestly. Ultimately, he places distance between
himself and others by habitually withdrawing or encouraging others to withdraw from him because they don't know
what makes him tick.

Passivity exacts a very high price physically. Researchers
have linked nonexpressiveness with higher cancer risks
and a shorter life.[12] Holding a feeling inside does not eradicate it. In fact, many negative feelings which are not expressed to the person who elicits them are carried home
and deposited on loved ones. Psychologists call this *displacement*. All of us have felt the ill effects of displacement
when we were harangued for some insignificant action and
then later found that this anger was engendered by someone else.

Compliant behavior does not necessarily bespeak a compliant attitude either. Sometimes passive persons choose
indirect ways to express their aggression. A young Korean
boy came into the employ of a group of American GIs
during the Korean War. The soldiers, weary from the rigors
of regimented army life, constantly played practical jokes
on their young helper. They would put peanut butter in his
shoes, short-sheet his bed, and send him on errands to
destinations which did not exist. The lad always responded
graciously to the GIs and maintained politeness in his conversation regardless of their high jinks. Finally, the soldiers
became convicted of their practical joking and agreed
among themselves to terminate this behavior. They called
their young helper and announced corporately that they
would no longer trick him as before. To this the young man
responded nonchalantly and in his broken English, "You
stop treating me bad anymore, I stop spitting in your soup."

Passivity, like aggression, is no way to resolve a conflict.
Although it seems more pleasant at first glance, the strate-

gy is fraught with pitfalls. It demands dishonesty or nonexpressiveness. It denies others the opportunity to learn from our observations. It distances us from others and can negatively affect our physical and emotional health.

Honestly Speaking

When I was a professor at a Christian college, I had a colleague with whom I always enjoyed spending time. We could discuss any topic—personal, political, spiritual, vocational—and he would share his honest opinions with me. Randy didn't always agree with me, but when he did, I never doubted his sincerity; and when he didn't agree, I clearly understood why. I found it very easy to share honestly with him as well and felt accepted, regardless of the positions I took or the feelings I shared. I came to ask for his observations regularly and found his input more valuable than opinions from others who told me what I wanted to hear.

Psychologists call such honest and forthright communication *assertiveness*. Assertive people are direct and clear. They are confident and feel in control of themselves. They are in touch with their feelings and take responsibility for themselves. Their goal is to communicate accurately, respecting both themselves and others. This may involve pointing out an area of conflict or of disappointment. However, it may also involve saying, "I love you." Assertiveness allows them to be honest—tactfully. They live by the dictum: You matter and so do I.

Assertiveness sometimes comes under fire in the Christian community because it is seen as violating the turn-the-other-cheek command of Christ. However, few Christians would say that Jesus advocated dishonesty. Indeed, He modeled clear and direct communication in every aspect of His ministry. He had no difficulty commending a Pharisee who answered Him wisely (Mark 12:34) or denouncing unrighteous Pharisees in the strongest terms (Matthew 23). He freely forgave a repentant Zaccheus for unfairly exacting taxes from his countrymen, but forcefully cleansed the temple area on two occasions of merchants who were profiting excessively from the worshipers. Jesus honestly confronted the woman at the well with her sinful lifestyle yet honestly forgave her and many others who repented of such a lifestyle. It's clear from Christ's actions that humility does not demand passivity and nonexpressiveness.

We all enjoy personal rights afforded us by God, due to our position as redeemed in Christ, and also by other people. And yet, some Christians teach that we have no rights, since we owe all to God. This teaching is tragic since it disenfranchises people of their privileges and tends to create a worthless-worm mentality. A more accurate view is that we enjoy many rights but may choose to waive them in the interest of spiritual or relational goals.

The Apostle Paul understood the rights issue. He recognized his position in Christ as well as his personal accomplishments and he frequently reminded others of both. He often waived his rights to further the development of his converts. For example, he abstained from eating meats which had been used in sacrifices before they were marketed, and he refused to receive support from the Corinthians while acting as their minister.

However, Paul could also be outspoken in demanding his rights. When he was arrested, jailed, and beaten in Philippi, he laid claim to his Roman citizenship. The officials then tried to usher him out the back door quietly, but he demanded an official public escort by the magistrates and received one (Acts 16). Paul later asserted his Roman citizenship (Acts 22) and demanded an audience with Caesar himself (Acts 25). He confronted Peter on charges of hypocrisy (Galatians 2) and appealed forcefully to believers everywhere who engaged in unrighteous behavior.

We enjoy many rights and must recognize these if we are to communicate honestly with others. We have the right to request things from others, although this doesn't necessarily mean all of our requests will be granted. People rebuked blind Bartimaeus for shouting his plea to Jesus, but his forthright request for mercy was answered by restored vision. If we don't ask, we may not receive.

We also have the right to refuse. Daniel decided to say no to the king's fine foods and God rewarded him for his stand.

We have the right to express our feelings and opinions without apology—even odd feelings and unusual opinions. We always have the right to waive any of our rights as well. However, we must ensure that we maintain our silence for a thoughtful reason, rather than for a fearful one.

Assertive people usually have good relationships because they don't force others to read their minds. We enjoy receiving honest answers to questions, sincere feedback on our performance, and heartfelt sharing of emotions from others. The adage "Honesty is the best policy" is especially true in conflict resolution because possible solutions are discussed in the light of clarity.

Steps in Conflict Resolution

The decision to adopt an assertive philosophy is the initial step in the process of effective conflict resolution. However, we must guide this openness to ensure tactful sharing and to produce optimal interpersonal results.

• Define the conflict. "My parents never want me to have fun," sneered fifteen-year-old Frank. "They hate me. That's why they make me stay home all afternoon and then see a shrink like you." Frank was not one of my happier patients, and he minced no words in conveying his complaints. His parents were at the end of their rope with him. "He's the most disrespectful boy I've ever seen," shouted Frank's father, "and I don't know how to make him straighten up and fly right!"

Using all of my professional judgment, I came to the learned conclusion that a parent-child conflict was living and breathing right in my office. So I quickly turned to Frank's mother and asked for her observations. She concisely diagnosed the problem: Frank was doing poorly in school so his father demanded that Frank do his homework immediately after school, before engaging in any other activities. This forced Frank to quit the football team which practiced at 3 P.M. He was angry about this and displayed it by sitting in front of his books as commanded but refusing to apply himself to his studies. She reported that her son and husband related well before this study arrangement was implemented.

I asked each family member to define the conflict. Frank said his father didn't want him to have fun anymore. His father declared that Frank was rebellious against all authority. Then I turned to Mrs. Rinehart. She succinctly stated, "They can't agree on a mutually acceptable time for Frank to do his homework." Bingo! Once father and son agreed with the wise mother's definition, study time was moved to 7 P.M. and everyone became happy. Would that all my cases were this easy!

Most readers can quickly define the conflict in the above illustration and may wonder why the males had so much trouble seeing the obvious. That's because they were warring with one another, never stopping to examine what they were really fighting about. Unfortunately, we all tend to lose objectivity when we're plaintiffs in a conflict. And when the combatants are the two spouses, there's no third party to analyze the situation calmly.

We must initiate the process of conflict resolution by precisely defining why we're disagreeing. It's astonishing how infrequently her definition agrees with his. She believes he only caresses her when he desires a sexual favor, and he sees the same set of circumstances as her insatiable desire to exercise control over him. This couple will disagree forever because neither is producing arguments that speak to the spouse's issues.

In marriage counseling I often interrupt a disagreement, hand each a sheet of paper, and ask them independently to write the crux of their disagreement. When they later trade papers, neither can believe what they are reading. No wonder they need marriage counseling; they don't even know what they've been fighting about for so long.

An excellent strategy for spouses is for the husband to describe as completely as possible his wife's view of the conflict until his wife agrees with the assessment. Then she must do the same until her husband can say that his perceptions were presented accurately. Each person is usually amazed at the partner's misconceptions. This process tends to diffuse conflict because it moves the adversaries from their naive convictions that they know exactly what the other is thinking. It provides either a common definition of the conflict or definitions of two separate conflicts which each demand individual attention.

• Identify your contributions. Now that we know what all the fuss is about, we can move toward resolution. The natural response is elaboration on our partner's blatant injustices which are perpetuating the conflict. "You always place your mother's wishes before mine." "The company can't grow while you insist on this outdated computer system." "You shouldn't interpret that Scripture passage so rigidly."

These words win us no medals, but rather promote defensiveness. A more strategic approach involves identifying our contribution to the problem first—even if that contribution is relatively small. Use the "I" messages described in chapter 8 and take full credit for your impropriety. "I have a bad attitude about your mother through which I filter all of your statements." "I don't like our computer system because I've had more experience with IBM computers and software." "I've struggled with legalism so much that I generally steer away from shackling interpretations of those verses."

• Listen to your partner's points. After defining the conflict and identifying my contributions to it, most problems seem much more resolvable than my initial perceptions indicated. Now you deserve an opportunity to explain your point of view. I hope you will follow my lead and identify your contributions to the conflict. Yours will certainly include some interpretations which differ from mine.

I should use the active listening skills described in chapter 10 to demonstrate full attention to your communication. Open ears and a healthy attitude may place me in a position to learn something!

• Identify options and choose a winner. When all parties understand each other, an action strategy for resolution is in order. We usually know what resolution we would like, and there is always a danger that we will present this as the *only* option or the *right* solution. Typically, there are multiple alternatives from which to choose and compromise positions which help us meet our partner halfway.

If the conflict is with your wife over her frequent invitations to her mother to visit, numerous outcomes are possible. Your favorite may be that she has used up all of her visits for the next five years. Your spouse may feel like her mother should move in permanently. Conflict definition reveals that you have a bad attitude about dear old Mom and that your spouse feels responsible to defend her mother. Other options include visits by your wife at her mother's house, coordinating Mom's visits at your house with your golf games, or devoting time to your mother-in-law in the interest of understanding her needs and appreciating her contributions to your mutual loved one. There's a good chance that these alternatives will be satisfying to all.

When We Receive No Cooperation
The rational steps just outlined work marvelously when your partner is equally interested in resolving a conflict as you are. Unfortunately, this is not always the case. Perhaps your adversary is unwilling to join you in the resolution process or you don't have a formal relationship with him that affords you the opportunity for prolonged discussion of the issues.

Suppose Robin, your neighbor, calls just before school dismisses and says, "There's a great sale going on at Macy's today. I've been cleaning my house all day and haven't taken time to get down there. I'd like to drop Karen by your house after school for a few hours while I shop. I'm sure you understand."

Maybe you do understand and would enjoy having seven-year-old Karen over for the afternoon while Robin shops. Then there's no conflict. But what if little Karen is quite a pistol, adept at disrupting your children's normal after-school routine of homework and chores? Maybe Karen doesn't play well with your children, and Robin requests free baby-sitting privileges from you several times a week. Besides, she's been home all day without Karen and has had ample opportunity to shop. You may still decide to keep Karen, as a friendly gesture, even though it will require schedule adjustments. That's your choice.

Suppose you do not wish to watch Karen and feel taken advantage of by Robin each time she calls with these last-minute requests. You envision the interpersonal struggles Karen's presence will precipitate with your kids and the disorganization that always ensues. Your subtle indications of inconvenience typically go unnoticed by Robin, who perseveres through any mild objection until she hears, "Sure. Bring Karen on over." You become angry with yourself for accepting the assignment and angry at Robin for asking repeatedly. However, you say nothing, instead choosing to avoid Robin whenever possible and complaining about her inconsiderateness.

You have the right to refuse this request and to resolve the conflict in a manner that protects your family, maintains your sanity, and does not reward Robin for being overbearing. However, this requires speaking up for yourself honestly.

Psychologists Jan Kelley and Barbara Winship have developed a three-part assertive response which allows you to be direct while maintaining sensitivity and tact.[13] I teach this strategy to hundreds of workshop participants and patients, with very favorable results.

• You begin with an empathy statement—an acknowledgment of the desires and opinions of the other person. As you place yourself in the other person's shoes, you demonstrate your interest in the person and your consideration of her circumstances. The empathy statement begins with the words, "I realize. . . ." To Robin you might say, "I realize that you are excited about the sale at Macy's." Another empathy statement would be, "I realize it's much more enjoyable to shop without Karen tagging along." There are many possibilities. The only criterion is that the statement conveys the point of view of the person to whom you're talking. Employing an empathy statement is the best way to win the other person's attention for the presentation of your own point of view.

• The next step is a content statement. This is the rationale for your own position stated as simply as possible. It begins, "However. . . ." To Robin you might offer the following content statement, "However, I want my children to concentrate on their homework after school today." You want to be as clear as possible in your content statement, but you need not become bogged down in details. One sentence incorporating the pronoun "I" is most desirable.

• The final part of the response is an action statement— a declaration of exactly what you want (or don't want). Initiate action statements with "Therefore. . . ." An action statement to Robin might be, "Therefore, I'm not able to keep Karen today." The action statement must be clear. "Therefore, I'm not sure if it would be a good idea for Karen to come over," is too weak and open for argument. If Robin is adept at ignoring the wishes of others in favor of her own, she will have little difficulty countering this suggestion.

The action statement must also be concise. You are responsible for indicating your own desires, not for generating twenty possible solutions for the other person. Avoid statements such as, "You could try calling Sue or check in with your mother. I'll bet Karen would enjoy the story hour at the library downtown, or she might even have fun shopping with you." The more words you use, the less effective you become.

The three-part response is equally effective for making requests. Suppose you purchase a garment in a department store and upon closer inspection at home, discover a defect. When you take it back to the store, the salesperson informs you that since the garment was on sale, it cannot be returned. You can resolve the conflict by saying, "Thank you" and placing the clothing in the trashbin on the way back to your car, or you can attempt a more personally satisfying resolution.

Recognizing that the management of any retail establishment lives by the motto, "The customer is always right," your task should not be difficult. Looking directly at the salesperson and in a pleasant tone you might say, "I realize that you don't typically take returns on your sale merchandise. However, I found a ripped seam in this shirt only after I took it home. Therefore, I'd like to exchange it for a nondefective one." Since your request is reasonable and the return isn't being made for a whimsical reason, the salesperson will probably comply. If not, you should state the three-part response once more. If this still does not result in the desired transaction, there's a good probability that repeating it to the manager will prove more satisfying. Notice that you blame no one, you don't get angry, and you never raise your voice. This frees the store personnel to meet your requests without "losing."

The three-part assertive response is an effective way to manage conflict with persons who are not cooperative or with those you really don't know very well. It can also be used with close friends and family members when your usual methods of resolving differences break down.

TWELVE

"Listen to advice and accept instruction,
and in the end you will be wise."
Proverbs 19:20

When You Need
More Help

A Multitude of Counselors

To some people, seeking assistance from others to resolve their emotional concerns seems like admitting defeat, but there is strong biblical precedent for finding help outside of themselves. Their initial consultation should be with God. The Scriptures implore us to call upon our Heavenly Father, to come to the Son when we are weary and heavy laden, and to rely on the counsel of the Holy Spirit. We do this through prayer, meditation, and diligent study of the Scriptures.

The wise King Solomon was an ardent advocate of soliciting the counsel of others. In Proverbs 19:20 he implored, "Listen to advice and accept instruction, and in the end you will be wise." He also reiterated the importance of seeking guidance and surrounding oneself with an abundance of counselors for safety. The New Testament Epistles are replete with admonitions for believers to build one another up through encouragement and to bear the burdens of fellow Christians. These instructions would hardly be necessary if God did not expect us to share our hardships with our siblings in Christ.

Our most trusted friends are the logical human counselors to approach first. A devoted spouse, loving parents, or an encouraging neighbor may offer emotional support and good advice. People who have coped with trials similar to those facing us may be in the position to counsel us through a crisis. Sometimes it is encouraging just to know that others are concerned for our well-being.

The quality of guidance from our associates depends in great measure on the effort we devote to developing a personal support network. Yet, even when we are very diligent in cultivating relationships, we sometimes need more help, because our friends can advise us only to their levels of experience and competence.

When We Need a Professional Consult
The decision to seek services from a professional counselor is difficult for people who have never seen a mental health professional and are scared by the very prospect of looking. They may be unclear as to what constitutes a valid reason for initiating counseling. On their first appointments some people apologize to me for taking my time to discuss their emotional struggles. They believe that only major mental illnesses qualify for professional help.

Many people who are well adjusted enter counseling for growth experiences and to expand their horizons. Some come to the therapist's office to learn new skills or to discover their strengths. But most people who seek professional help are encountering personal issues which they cannot handle alone.

Any psychological difficulty which interferes with normal functioning, and stubbornly resists sincere efforts to remedy it, presents a valid reason to seek expert assistance. Professional help is particularly indicated when the person has little or no motivation to attack the problem and when attempts at spiritual solutions seem to go nowhere. Counselors can offer hope that improvement is possible. They can instill confidence and provide energy to get the ball rolling. Professional helpers can also provide new perspectives on the struggles, as they describe difficult circumstances from vantage points which may not have occurred to the person.

But Which Professional Do I Choose?

The decision to seek counseling is only the first step in getting professional assistance. Next, one must choose a therapist with whom to work. This may be a tricky task, since there are so many people who hold themselves out to be professional helpers, with titles ranging from palm reader to psychologist, and services ranging from worthless to life-changing. To whom should one turn?

• The question of values. One of the most important considerations is the value system under which you operate. Counseling is not a value-free venture. The moral, ethical, and spiritual values of both the helper and the help seeker play a vital role in the progress of therapy and the outcome of the process.

Values influence the definition of the problem on which therapy focuses. The value system of the emotional helper makes a tremendous difference in the way he defines the problem and the methods he uses to attack it. One counselor may view an unwanted pregnancy as an unfortunate accident remediable by the abortive knife of a surgeon, while another may see the predicament as a consequence of sexual choices with which the client must now cope. An adviser may encourage termination of church attendance to ease the guilt which accompanies an abortion, while another counselor may suggest viewing this emotion as a signal to consider the righteousness of the client's current lifestyle. Values determine the course of psychotherapy.

Some counselors purport to assist their clients without imposing their own values in the process, but I believe that this is impossible. The therapy goals agreed upon reflect the counselor's sentiments, and even the incidents the therapist inquires into represent a value judgment. It is imperative that you choose a professional helper who shares your values so you can enter the process without reservation.

• The specialties. The next decision involves which kind of professional to select. The choices are many. Merely browsing through the yellow pages under headings such as "counselors," "mental health clinicians," or "psychotherapists" is sure to confuse most persons. The following brief descriptions of some professional helpers will acquaint you with some of the resources available.

Pastors are on the front lines of the helping profession. They are often the first persons turned to in times of emotional upheaval. Most pastors have a rather brief seminary training in counseling and an abundance of on-the-job training. However, special programs in pastoral counseling are springing up in seminaries and some pastors are specializing in this ministry. Pastors should be considered when one's primary problem is of a spiritual nature and when matters of biblical interpretation are the focus of concern. Pastoral counselors usually offer services to individuals and families. Their practices may be regulated by their denominational agencies.

Psychologists provide a wide variety of psychological services including individual, group, marital, and family therapy and testing. Although psychologists are employed in diverse settings, most work with people who are struggling with emotional concerns but who can maintain their place in the community. Psychologists usually hold a bachelor's degree in psychology as well as a master's and doctor's degree in this field. Their training involves years of supervised practical experience and demonstrated expertise in conducting research. The practice of psychology is regulated by every state, and practitioners are required to maintain a license to practice.

Psychiatrists are physicians who usually work with severely disturbed patients or those who need hospitalization. They are trained as medical doctors and specialize in psychiatry after completing their general medical education. Psychiatrists are licensed to prescribe medications for psychological maladies, and usually align themselves with a hospital practice.

The title *counselor* represents a mixed bag of care-givers with diverse specialties. In states where this title is regulated, practitioners usually hold master's degrees in counseling, and work under the supervision of a psychologist.

Their training includes course work and practical experience in counseling, and they tend to work with people who are not in need of hospitalization. In most states, however, the title is not regulated; and although many who use it fit the above description, others adopt the title without obtaining the necessary training or supervision.

Social workers specialize in helping people resolve problems within their social and family systems. They generally hold master's degrees in social work and their practice is regulated in some states. Historically, social workers worked closely with psychiatrists to provide therapy and assistance to people whose social system impaired their functioning.

Helpers adopt many other titles to identify their niche in the mental health field. Unfortunately there is little consensus on the level of expertise that these less familiar titles represent. For example, the title, *psychotherapist*, is not regulated in most states and can, therefore, be adopted by anyone. It generally connotes a trained psychologist or counselor but not always. Other titles such as *marriage facilitator*, *mental health clinician*, and *spiritual adviser* are even more vague. When considering practitioners with unfamiliar titles, be sure to ask adequate questions to determine their qualifications to offer any treatment.

● Practical considerations. Counseling usually involves many hours of talking with a helper as you develop a relationship and share ideas and feelings. Counseling sessions are held at regular intervals, normally on a weekly basis. Therefore, you should consider the location of your selected professional and the ease of scheduling and paying for regular meetings.

Fees for counseling services range from almost nothing to very expensive, and cost is a major issue in selecting a therapist. Some churches and religious organizations offer counseling services as a ministry and charge parishioners very little. Other churches provide these services, but charge a fee commensurate with the prevailing prices for professional services in the community. You can also find help at community mental health centers and college counseling centers at very reasonable rates, but your choice of counselors may be limited.

Practitioners who work in private or group practices offer the consumer freedom of choice but charge a somewhat higher fee for services. Health insurance policies typically offer outpatient psychotherapy benefits which help defray the cost of counseling significantly. These benefits will usually cover services rendered by licensed psychologists and psychiatrists and sometimes apply to licensed social workers and counselors as well.

It is wise to invest some time in choosing a therapist since their value systems, expertise, and fees differ so widely. Pastors are an excellent resource to get the process started because they are often familiar with the practitioners in the community who have a Christian commitment and who include a spiritual dimension in their treatments. Professional organizations such as the Christian Association for Psychological Studies (Box 628, Blue Jay, California 92317) publish membership directories which list Christian therapists by states. Graduate Christian counseling training programs such as the Psychological Studies Institute (2055 Mount Paran Road, Atlanta, Georgia 30327) also keep current listings of their graduates who have located all over the world.

Be a wise consumer. It is perfectly appropriate to ask questions about everything from the techniques used by the counselors to their fee schedules and payment expectations, *before* entering therapy. Ask about their training, spiritual commitments, and acceptance rates by health insurance carriers. All of these issues influence your choices and should be considered.

ENDNOTES

[1]Kurt Koffka, *Principles of Gestalt Psychology* (New York: Harcourt, Brace, and World, 1935).

[2]Berkeley Rice, "Imagination to Go," *Psychology Today* (May 1984), pp. 48–56.

[3]Stanley Schacter and Jerome Singer, "Cognitive, Social and Physiological Determinants of Emotional State," *Psychological Review* (vol. 69, 1962), pp. 379–99.

[4]Leon Festinger, *A Theory of Cognitive Dissonance* (Stanford: Stanford University Press, 1957).

[5]Kenneth Matheny and Richard Riordan, *Therapy American Style* (Chicago: Nelson-Hall, 1979).

[6]Logan Wright, "The Type A Behavior Pattern in Coronary Artery Disease: Quest for the Active Ingredient and the Elusive Mechanism," *American Psychologist* (vol. 43, 1988), pp. 2–14.

[7]Eleanor Smith, "Fighting Cancerous Feelings," *Psychology Today* (May 1988), pp. 21–23.

[8]Howard L. Millman, Jack T. Huber, and Dean R. Diggins, *Therapies for Adults* (San Francisco: Jossey-Bass, 1982).

⁹M.A. Schlesser and K.Z. Altshuler, "The Genetics of Affective Disorder: Data, Theory and Clinical Application," *Hospital and Community Psychiatry* (vol. 34, 1983), pp. 415–22.

¹⁰See the following sources:

H. Anisman and R.M. Zacharko, "Depression: The Predisposing Influence of Stress," *The Behavioral and Brain Sciences* (vol. 5, 1982), pp. 89–137.

G.C. Davidson and J.M. Neale, *Abnormal Psychology: An Experimental Clinical Approach* (3rd edition) (New York: Wiley, 1982).

¹¹John H. Greist, Marjorie H. Klein, Roger R. Eischens, John Faris, Alan S. Gurman, and William P. Morgan, "Running as a Treatment for Depression," *Comprehensive Psychiatry* (vol. 20, 1979), pp. 41–54.

¹²Smith, "Cancerous Feelings."

¹³Jan Kelley and Barbara Winship, *I Am Worth It* (Chicago: Nelson-Hall, 1979).